The
GLASS
CEILING

The
GLASS
CEILING

A Look at Women in the Workforce

Ann E. Weiss

TWENTY-FIRST CENTURY BOOKS
Brookfield, Connecticut

For Margot and Rebecca

Library of Congress Cataloging-in-Publication Data
Weiss, Ann E., 1943–
The glass ceiling: a look at women in the workforce
p. cm.
Includes bibliographical references and index.
Summary: Considers women in the workforce throughout history and the
development of a "glass ceiling" that keeps them from rising to high levels
in many corporations.
ISBN 0-7613-1365-6 (lib. bdg.)
1. Discrimination in employment—United States—Juvenile literature. 2. Women
executives—United States—Juvenile literature. 3. Sex discrimination in employment—United States—Juvenile literature. 4. Women—Promotions—United
States—Juvenile literature. 5. Sex discrimination against women—United States—
Juvenile literature. [1.Women—Employment. 2. Sex discrimination against women.
3. Sex discrimination in employment. 4. Discrimination in employment.] I. Title.
HD6054.4.U6W42 1999
331.4'133'0973—dc21   98-39822
                                                                            CIP
                                                                            AC

Published by Twenty-First Century Books
A Division of The Millbrook Press, Inc.
2 Old New Milford Road
Brookfield, Connecticut 06804

CONTENTS

A GLASS CEILING?

"I got the best job there was," Madeline Hennessey Mertens says now. "The best job there was."

That was back in 1930. Madeline Mertens—still Madeline Hennessey in those days—had just been hired to teach kindergarten at the Nash School in Augusta, Maine. The pay didn't amount to much: $500 a year. But the young woman loved the work. "It was the best kindergarten in the city of Augusta," she remembers. "I looked forward to seeing thirty-five little faces every September."

Madeline Hennessey didn't get to look forward to many new September classes. In 1937 she married Henry Mertens, and her teaching career came to an abrupt end. "I had to leave," she explained to a news reporter sixty years later. "They didn't allow people to teach after they were married."

They didn't allow *women* to teach after they were married. That's what Madeline Mertens meant. Under Maine law as it stood in the 1930s, only single women could work full-time in the state's public schools. Once a woman had a husband to "support" her financially, it was assumed that she no longer needed a salary of her own. A married woman might therefore be required to "step aside" so that a man—presumably with a wife of his own to support—could take her job. Although Madeline Mertens was occasionally allowed back into the classroom as a substitute teacher, she considers her last day at the Nash School her last day of teaching. Even now, it saddens her to think of it.[1]

Things certainly changed in the six decades after the law forced Madeline Mertens into early retirement! By the 1990s, women— married, single, divorced, separated, with children and without— made up about 45 percent of the workforce in the United States.

Women in Government and Business

One of those working women was Madeleine K. Albright. In January 1997 President Bill Clinton appointed Albright as his secretary of state. With that, she became the first woman to head the U.S. State Department. The State Department is the section of the federal government responsible for handling U.S. relations with other countries. The secretary of state is a member—some would say the leading member—of the presidential "cabinet," the group of people who direct the various federal departments and act as a president's closest official advisors. In the two hundred and eight years since President George Washington appointed his first cabinet in 1789, sixty-two men—and not one woman—had served as secretary of state. Now that had changed.

Yet by 1997 it seemed less remarkable to see a female secretary of state than it would have just a few years earlier. Before 1987, only nine women had ever been named to the U.S. cabinet.[2] The first, Frances Perkins, was chosen as secretary of labor by President Franklin D. Roosevelt in 1933. It took twenty years for a second woman to reach the cabinet level of government, and twenty-four *more* for a third to follow. But in 1997 President Clinton's fourteen-member cabinet boasted four women. In addition to Madeleine Albright, there were Attorney-General Janet Reno, Secretary of Labor Alexis M. Herman, and Secretary of Health and Human Services Donna E. Shalala.

Women are making gains in elected politics, as well. Take the U.S. Congress, the nation's chief lawmaking body. Before 1948 no woman had ever served in the Senate, the "upper house" of Congress. In 1997 there were nine female senators. Add in the fifty-odd female members of the U.S. House of Representatives, the "lower house," for a total of nearly sixty women in Congress. Women were also making headway in state and local government. The United States had two female governors as of November 1997 and numerous female state lawmakers, mayors, city council members, and the like.[3] It's a similar story in Canada, where about 14 percent of Parliament, the national legislature, was female in the mid-1990s.[4]

In business, too, women are making strides into what was once considered a man's world. In the mid-1980s, Katherine Graham, owner of *The Washington Post* newspaper, was the sole female chief executive officer (CEO) of a Fortune 500 company. (The business magazine *Fortune* ranks businesses according to their size and value. A Fortune 500 company is one of the nation's 500 largest businesses. A Fortune 100 company is one of the hundred largest, and so on.) Although Katherine Graham was a distinguished publisher and business leader, she owed her executive position to the fact that her father had bought the *Post* in 1933.[5] But by the 1990s, women were becoming company vice presidents and CEOs on the strength of their own accomplishments. In 1992 Jill Barad became the first female got-there-on-her-own CEO of a Fortune 500 business. Barad worked her way to the top at Mattel, the toy company.[6]

Other Women in the Workplace

Women are succeeding in other fields. America's manned space program was all-male during its first nineteen years. Finally, in 1978 officials at the National Aeronautics and Space Administration (NASA) selected six women as candidates for space travel. Five years later, Sally Ride became the first of the six to blast off.[7]

Today, women are continuing their space adventure. In 1996 fifty-three-year-old Shannon Lucid spent more than half a year living and working aboard the Russian space station *Mir*. The next year, Americans by the thousands watched as dramatic photos of the planet Mars unfolded on their home computer screens. Many of the photos included images of a small, self-powered, and self-guided roving vehicle called Sojourner. Sojourner was designed by NASA's Donna L. Shirley.[8]

Dr. Shirley is an engineer as well as head of NASA's Jet Propulsion Laboratory in Pasadena, California. Sally Ride is not only an astronaut but also a physicist. Shannon Lucid is a biochemist. Biochemistry, physics, and engineering are just some of the sciences welcoming women today. Women work as dentists, family doctors, surgeons, and medical researchers. They are astronomers and oceanographers, mathematicians, and computer programmers. It was a woman, Karen Kare, who designed such familiar Macintosh computer icons as the smiley-faced monitor and the little trash can that bulges comically when you "put" something in it.[9]

Actually, Karen Kare's background is not in computer technology but in the arts. In the arts and entertainment fields, as in the sciences, women are increasingly making their presence known. And not just in such traditionally feminine roles as singers, dancers, and actresses, either. In 1996 Jamie Tarses became president of ABC-TV's Entertainment Division. Tarses was the first woman to hold such a high position at any major television network. Women's paintings and sculptures hang in museums and galleries. Women write best-selling books and attention-grabbing music. They conduct symphony orchestras.

Women can be found throughout the workforce today. They serve in the armed forces, with the police, and as firefighters. Those with a religious calling may become ministers or rabbis. Female athletes have won international recognition in tennis, ice hockey, golf, basketball, and gymnastics. Women certainly have come a long way since Madeline Hennessey Mertens was forced out of her kindergarten classroom all those years ago. It seems as if there's *nothing* that modern working women cannot accomplish.

Not so fast! some women say. They, and many men as well, believe that there are many things that women cannot do—or are not allowed to do—in the workplace. As they see it, women like Jamie Tarses and Sally Ride are the exception, not the rule. For every Tarses or Ride, there are dozens of other working women who find it impossible to rise as far as they would like to in their chosen fields. These women feel as if they are being held down by an invisible, but powerful, barrier that keeps them from reaching the top. Many call this barrier the "glass ceiling."

Glass Ceiling—Yes or No?

Is there a glass ceiling for women in the workplace? Yes. That, at least, is the opinion of the authors of a 1987 study sponsored by The Center for Creative Leadership in Greensboro, North Carolina. The center is dedicated to researching business management issues.

According to that study, working men are generally judged, paid, and promoted according to their individual abilities. Working women are not. Instead, the authors say, "women as a group . . . are kept from advancing higher *because they are women*."[10] Being kept from advancement means more than just having to settle for an unimpressive-sounding job title, the authors assert. It means that women are paid less than men. They may even be paid less for doing exactly the same kind of work. In fact, a 1997 U.S. government survey showed that women who work full-time earn just 75 cents for every dollar earned by full-time working men.[11]

Others pooh-pooh the notion of a glass ceiling. Things are different now than when The Center for Creative Leadership published its study, they say. Maybe there really was a glass ceiling in 1987, but not anymore. "The glass ceiling has certainly been shattered," Sheila E. Widnall told a women's group in 1997. For her, it certainly has. Widnall is secretary of the U.S. Air Force—the first woman to hold that position.[12]

Widnall is not the only one who feels that the glass ceiling is a thing of the past. Today's young women have just as many opportunities as their male counterparts, argues a group called the Independent Women's Forum. Forum leaders maintain that by some measurements, women's salaries almost exactly equal men's.[13] We'll look at the conflicting pay statistics more closely in chapter 5.

Still other opinions fall somewhere between the two extremes. "Perhaps the ceiling is more like plastic than glass," muses one woman in the publishing industry. "You can push your way through into the soft plastic and look at the higher levels of management, but never break through. And how seriously do your fellow workers take you?" She and many others concede that things have changed since 1987. But by how much?

Certainly, a few female athletes have won fame and fortune on the tennis courts and the balance beam. But what are a woman's chances of playing in the big-league team sports where male athletes regularly sign multimillion-dollar contracts? Yes, there are some women ministers and rabbis, but virtually all of the most influential religious leaders are male. A few women have made it to the top, or close to it, in business and the professions. Overall, though, they represent only a tiny fraction of the individuals at those levels. Studies show that women account for only about 3 percent of executive management at Fortune 500 companies.[14] And don't forget that Sheila Widnall is the *only* woman who has served as secretary of a branch of the U.S. armed services.

As for politics: according to *The New York Times*, the Canadian government ranks twenty-first in the world in terms of female participation. Put more simply, there are twenty countries in which women play a larger role in government than they do in Canada. The United States, however, is not one of them. The percentage of U.S. women in government leaves the United States in forty-first place worldwide.[15]

Surprised? Think about it. A record-breaking nine women in the U.S. Senate *still* leaves that body 91 percent male!

So is there a glass ceiling or isn't there? Are women really treated unfairly at work? If so, why? If there is a glass ceiling, how did it get there? What keeps it in place? Does it affect all working women—nurse's aides, surgeons, executive vice presidents, factory workers, day-care providers? And most important of all: If the glass ceiling does exist, what is the best way to go about shattering it?

2

A LOOK BACK

Snaps and snails and puppy-dogs' tails, that's what little boys are made of. Of course. And little girls? *Sugar and spice and everything nice.*

Boys and girls are very, very different. That's the message our society, and the Western European cultures upon which our society is largely based, have traditionally passed down from generation to generation. Even in nursery rhymes, we define girls as sweet, soft, and gentle. Boys are feisty and tough. They are gritty and adventurous, well-suited to assume their future responsibility of protecting and providing for the "weaker sex."

There is another difference between boys—and men—and girls and women. The former are more valuable than the latter.

Literally more valuable, worth more money. In the Bible, in the Old Testament book of Leviticus, God tells the Hebrew leader Moses that the value of a male infant is to be set at five shekels of silver. A female baby is worth three shekels. A grown man's value is fifty shekels; a woman's, thirty. For children and young adults, the male-female distinction is even greater. Boys between the ages of five and twenty are worth twenty shekels; girls are worth just half as much.[1]

The Hebrews were not the only ancient people who considered women less valuable than men. According to the Greek philosopher Aristotle, who lived from 384 to 322 B.C., "The male is by nature superior, and the female inferior." When Aristotle used the words "by nature," he meant that female inferiority was a built-in fact of human life. Nothing could change that. "This principle . . . ," he noted, "extends to all mankind."[2] To Aristotle, women were like children—or slaves. "The poor, not having slaves," he wrote, "must employ both their women and children as servants." Nearly three hundred years later, the Roman statesman, writer, and orator Marcus Tullius Cicero weighed in with his opinion. Because of their "weakness of intellect," Cicero declared, women should be placed under the guardianship of men. Other Roman men, citing women's "ignorance of business matters," agreed that they needed looking after.[3]

Where did it come from, this idea that women are inferior to—and worth less than—men? Remember the Bible story of the creation of the world and the temptation of Eve by the serpent in the Garden of Eden. Eve listens to the serpent, disobeys God, and eats the forbidden fruit. She even shares the fruit with Adam, her husband. For their sin, Adam and Eve and all their human descendants are banished from the Garden. They were condemned by God to live and work "in sorrow" forevermore. But because it was Eve who first tasted the fruit and persuaded Adam to do likewise, women were doubly punished. They became subservient to their husbands. "He [your husband] shall rule over thee," God tells Eve. The Old Testament, with its particular view of women, helps form the basis of belief for three of the world's major religions: Judaism, Christianity, and Islam.

Widespread belief in the story of Adam and Eve helps explain why so many people, in so many different times and places, have regarded women as inferior to men. It's not the whole explanation, though. Surely Aristotle and Cicero were not influenced by Bible writings. In any case, the human race is far older than the Old Testament. Ideas about men and women, and the differences between them, must reach far back into prehistoric times. How were women regarded in all the thousands of years before recorded history?

Women in Prehistory

To try to answer that question, we look to archaeology, the study of long-ago people through the material objects that those people left behind. When the remains of prehistoric humans were first discovered in the mid-1800s, archaeologists used them to construct a picture of how early people lived. The bones of prehistoric males often were found alongside stone knives, arrowheads, or axes. Archaeologists had no trouble figuring out what that meant. Prehistoric men had designed the tools with which they made their first crude weapons. Armed with those weapons, they ventured forth in search of game—lions, bears, and elk. Then they brought their kill back to the dwelling place to share with the women and children.

What were prehistoric women doing while the men were out hunting for food? The archaeologists studied the evidence—female skeletons accompanied by scatterings of beads and shells—and came up with an answer. Women spent most of their time in or near the group home, caring for their children. They probably gathered roots and nuts, and may have tended a few fruit-bearing plants. Sometimes they received gifts, bracelets and necklaces of beads and shells, from the men in the group.

Women had lower status than men even in prehistory, the archaeologists concluded, and no wonder. From the very start, men were the givers of gifts, the suppliers of food, the makers of tools. Men did more for the group than women did, and their larger contribution earned them a superior place within the group. That was the meaning of what they were finding in prehistoric graves, the archaeologists agreed. Males were honored by being buried with the valuable implements they invented and used. Females were laid to rest with the bits of jewelry with which their men adorned them.

Proof enough that female inferiority is, as Aristotle put it, "natural" to all humanity.

What's wrong with this picture? asks Margaret Ehrenberg, a present-day British archaeologist. Her answer: plenty.

To begin with, Ehrenberg points out, the remains studied by early archaeologists are just that: remains. They are objects that have survived over tens of thousands of years, hard objects like bones, minerals, and shells. Who is to say that prehistoric women weren't buried with items as numerous—and as valuable—as men were? The food those women cooked, the skins and furs they turned into clothing, the baskets they wove, the utensils they made and used, all may have been placed in their graves with them. If so, that would indicate that the contributions of prehistoric women were considered valuable after all. But many of the objects likely to have been buried with women were made of soft, organic (once living) materials. Food and fur, wooden spoons, and reed baskets are quicker to rot away than are inorganic minerals or even bone. They are also less likely to survive the farmer's plow or the scavenging of animals. So, Ehrenberg argues, no one can conclude, simply by studying grave sites, that prehistoric men regarded women as inferior to themselves.[4] In fact, she continues, other evidence suggests that the sexes may well have enjoyed equality in prehistoric days. This evidence is anthropological.

Ehrenberg is an anthropologist as well as an archaeologist. As an anthropologist, she has studied many human cultures, their origins, customs, and beliefs.

Ehrenberg points out that there are still a few twentieth-century groups whose way of life resembles that of prehistoric people. Among such "hunter-gatherers," women are every bit as important as men in providing food. The !Kung women of the Kalahari Desert in southwest Africa, for instance, gather not just fruits and vegetables, but roots, bulbs, tubers, eggs, and such small wildlife as lizards, turtles, and insects. These foods make up 60 to 80 percent of the !Kung diet. In remote parts of Australia, tribeswomen hunt kangaroos and other game with the help of dogs they have trained themselves.[5] Among the Hidatsa, a now-extinct Native American group of the Great Plains, men and women shared all food-related tasks except for the killing and butchering of animals.[6]

Even in nonhuman societies, the sexes may divide food-gathering jobs more or less equally. The great apes, our closest relatives in the animal world, do just that. Similar sharing was a feature of early human societies as well, says Sally Slocum, also an anthropologist. Ehrenberg further questions the assumption that meat was as central to the prehistoric diet as some believe. Stone axes would hardly have been effective against such large creatures as elk and bear, she points out. Much early "hunting" probably consisted of men and women happening across an animal killed by nonhuman predators and ripping flesh from its carcass.[7]

Why, then, did the archaeologists of the nineteenth century insist that prehistoric men were big-game hunters and the primary suppliers of food? Ehrenberg suggests that these archaeologists made the mistake of judging the prehistoric evidence according to the standards and beliefs of their own time.

Virtually without exception, the early archaeologists were European and American men from the educated middle- and upper-classes. They lived in societies in which men were the bread-winners, and women were not expected to work outside the home unless poverty forced them to do so. Girls were less well educated than boys. They were barred from going to college, receiving a degree, or training to enter a profession. In the world as these archaeologists knew it, men owned nearly all the wealth, sharing it, often in the form of gifts of jewelry, with their wives and daughters. Hunting was a sport of the aristocracy. It was a "manly" pastime, off-limits to women. "No one would have questioned whether [prehistoric] men, rather than women, were the hunters," Ehrenberg says.[8] For the most part, no one questioned the other assumptions of early archaeologists.

Today's archaeologists don't just question the old assumptions. Most dismiss them altogether, agreeing that the men and women of prehistory probably did share equally in the tasks of daily living. But if that is true, when did the sharing stop? And why? What happened that led so many men of the ancient world—Aristotle, Cicero, and the Old Testament scribes among them—to make such disdainful assumptions about women?

A Growing Inequality

Ehrenberg suggests that the answer can be summed up in one word: agriculture. Modern agriculture probably got its start eight thousand or more years ago in the fertile valley of the Nile River, in what is now Egypt. Over the ages, it spread into Asia and Europe. Agriculture may not have reached the northwesternmost parts of Europe until as late as 1000 B.C.

Modern agriculture is different from the simple plant cultivation common among prehistoric people or today's hunter-gatherers. That sort of cultivation requires little more than a sunny patch of earth and one person wielding a stick or hoe. Agriculture, by contrast, demands heavy equipment, like metal plows, and large tracts of land. It calls for strong workers, and plenty of them.

The new demands of agriculture had powerful consequences— "unforeseen, and unfortunate," Ehrenberg calls them—for women. With the increased need for workers, it became the responsibility of women to supply those workers. Bearing children, and rearing them, would now have been seen as a woman's "major role," Ehrenberg says. As women became increasingly occupied with pregnancy and child care, they would have had less time than in the past to contribute to food gathering. And as Ehrenberg reminds us, this contribution had been "a crucial factor in maintaining the equal status they [women] had previously enjoyed."[9] Thus, even as modern European societies were emerging, those societies had come to value women less for themselves and the work they performed than for their ability to produce and raise each new generation of males.

And yet, say historians Bonnie S. Anderson and Judith P. Zinsser, the "vast majority of European women" have always assumed responsibilities beyond motherhood. Most have worked for money, either in the home, or outside it. Peasant women planted gardens, weeded them, harvested them, and sold the produce. They raised animals, and marketed eggs, chickens, meat, milk, wool, and the like. They made and sold butter and cheese. They wove cloth and sewed clothing; they spun yarn and knitted it; they fashioned delicate lace. Then they sold their wares door-to-door or brought them to town to hawk in the streets. They cleaned the homes of wealthier folk, did their laundry, and cared for their children.[10] Single young women often went into domestic service and worked for years to earn the money for the dowry that would enable them to marry and establish their own homes.

Europe's Working Women

Peasants were not Europe's only "working women." Throughout most of recorded history, European women of all classes have performed most of the same tasks that European men have. Men might be kings; women were queens. In tenth-century England, Aethelflaed, daughter of one king and widow of another, won the allegiance of noblemen beyond her own lands, thereby adding to the realm she had inherited from her husband.[11] Two earlier English queens, Ine and Cynethyth, minted coins in their own names, an indication of their political power.[12] During the mid-1400s, Margaret of Anjou, wife of King Henry VI of England, raised troops and money to defend her husband against his enemies. She helped Henry hold his throne for nearly twenty years.[13] In 1474 a twenty-three-year-old Castilian princess named Isabella seized control of the royal treasury and declared herself queen. Isabella was already married to King Ferdinand II of neighboring Aragon. With her husband, she was a driving force behind the unification of the two kingdoms and the creation of the modern nation of Spain.[14] In 1492, Queen Isabella bade farewell to Christopher Columbus as he set off on his voyage of discovery to the New World. Isabella of Castile, Margaret of Anjou, and the others are only a few of scores of European queens.

Some of those queens were warriors, as well. Margaret of Anjou did more than just raise troops. She also gave them their marching orders. Hundreds of years earlier, in A.D. 60, the British chieftain Boudicca led a revolt against the army of Rome, which had occupied much of Britain over the previous century. In her final, losing, battle against the Roman legions, Boudicca led a fighting force estimated to have numbered more than 100,000.[15] The queens Ine and Cynethyth went into battle to retain or extend the lands they ruled with their husbands.

But perhaps the most famous female soldier of all was France's Jeanne d'Arc. Jeanne was sixteen years old when, in 1428, she announced that God had called upon her to lead the French forces against that land's English invaders. (At the time, France and England had been at war for nearly a hundred years.) Dressed like a man, and armed like one, Jeanne charged fearlessly into battle on at least seven occasions. She was wounded, but survived to achieve her goal of escorting the rightful French king, Charles VII, to his coronation in the great cathedral city of Rheims.[16]

By no means were all female soldiers commanders. Thousands marched with the ranks. According to historians Anderson and Zinsser, up to one-quarter of those serving in the European armies of the thirteenth to the sixteenth centuries were women. Such women are customarily described as "camp followers"—a polite way of saying "prostitutes." In reality, however, these women performed a variety of tasks essential to any army. They dug trenches and latrines, collected fuel, cooked, and washed and mended clothing. They nursed the sick and wounded, and comforted the dying.

They buried the dead.[17] Today, such jobs are done by regular members of the armed services.

As soldiers, women did their part helping to kill and destroy. But women were also builders. At about the time Jeanne d'Arc was setting out for Rheims with Charles VII, German and Czechoslovakian women were mining ore and working in heavy construction. "Women carried stones, brought water for the mortar mixers, bunched thatch for roofs, collected moss and bracken to cushion the roof tiles of houses," Anderson and Zinsser write. Women helped build the cathedral in Siena, Italy, in 1336. Between 1365 and 1371, they dug ditches and carried stones and bricks for the construction of a college in Toulouse, France.[18]

Women could also earn money at less onerous jobs. Many were skilled in such crafts as thread- and silkmaking, woodworking, silversmithing, and so forth. Their skills enabled them to join a guild, an association of workers who specialized in a particular field. Of the two hundred craft guilds listed in Paris tax records for the year 1300, eighty or ninety accepted women as members. Guilds that accepted members of both sexes were commonly devoted to metal, wood-making, and leather-making. Twelve of the two hundred were exclusively female. Cologne, Germany, boasted forty guilds in 1397. Twenty-eight of them were open to women; three were all-female.[19] Guilds limited to women might produce textiles or finished clothing.

Some women went into business as merchants or moneylenders. The wives of wealthy landowners shouldered the task of running huge estates when their husbands were off at court or at war. Margaret Paston, who lived in fifteenth-century England, described the duties that fell to her when her husband was away. She settled disputes among the tenants of the estate, hired and supervised laborers, marketed the crops, bought weapons, sold timber, and arranged to borrow money when necessary. Besides all that, she successfully defended the property against armed attack.[20]

Women in the Arts

European women also found a place for themselves in the world of art and literature. The French Christine de Pisan (also spelled Pizan) was a writer and courtier, an attendant at the royal court. Christine was born in about 1364 and widowed at the age of twenty-three. For years she supported herself, her two children, an aging mother, and other relatives by writing. In manuscripts like *The Book of the City of Ladies*, Christine protested eloquently against the labeling of women as unintelligent or inferior to men. Christine also wrote poetry. Her last poem, which appeared in 1429, commemorated Jeanne d'Arc's victory over the English.[21]

Another female writer, Hildegard von Bingen, was born in Germany in 1098. When Hildegard was eight, she was sent to a Roman Catholic convent to be educated. Still in her teens, Hildegard took her vows as a nun and later became abbess (head) of her convent. She was known for her visions, which Church leaders, including the pope himself, accepted as divinely inspired. Popes and kings alike employed Hildegard on diplomatic missions. She was skilled with herbs, and wrote about their usefulness in healing. In addition, she produced plays and poetry, composed music (currently available in music stores and through a Hildegard site on the World Wide Web), and directed the illustration of her own manuscripts. In 1152, Hildegard left the convent where she had been raised and founded her own monastery.[22]

So well-known and well-loved was Hildegard von Bingen during her lifetime that immediately after her death in 1179, her admirers launched a campaign to have her declared a saint. The campaign failed, and over time Hildegard and her works faded from people's memories. Only in the last years of the twentieth century has she been rediscovered.

How could so gifted a person have been forgotten? Hildegard was a woman. As such, she was not expected to have a successful "career." For all her accomplishments, she was—as religion, philosophy, and custom made clear—an inferior being. Easy enough then, after her death, for new generations of male philosophers and scholars to dismiss her works as inferior, as well. Easy enough to forget her very existence.

The story of Hildegard von Bingen—a lifetime of accomplishment dismissed and forgotten—is the story of most European women over the ages. Of course we remember a handful of names like Jeanne d'Arc or Isabella of Spain. But few of us realize that so many women—their names long forgotten—wrote literature, participated in religious and political disputes, waged war, managed great estates, joined guilds, sold their wares, built cathedrals, and all the rest. If we think of these bygone women at all, we tend to lump them all together in a single category: wives and mothers. Most of them *were* wives and mothers, of course, but most were much more besides. Yet their accomplishments as working women have always been undervalued.

Women and Property

Again, "undervalued" is to be taken literally. Women's work has uniformly been considered worth less than men's. Female construction workers in fourteenth-century Italy were paid seven soldi a day. Males doing the same work took home fifteen soldi.[23] Fourteenth-century women who weeded the gardens of one French monastery received one-eighth the pay of the men who mowed the fields. A 1563 English law set the wages of women farmworkers at one-third to one-half those of men, even though both worked the same hours at equally hard jobs. "Whatever the task, wherever the place, whatever the century," say Bonnie Anderson and Judith Zinsser, "when it came to her wages, a woman earned one-third to one-half less than a boy or man."[24]

Even that meager wage did not necessarily belong to the woman who had worked for it. A married peasant woman would probably have turned over every penny she made to her husband, the head of the household. Even women of the wealthier classes were seen more as "helping out" a husband than as working to enrich or advance themselves. The lady who ran the manor while her husband was elsewhere was merely a surrogate, a substitute. The estate she managed did not belong to her. When its true owner returned home, she handed the reins of power back to him. Women warriors like Ine and Cynethyth fought to preserve their husbands' lands, not their own. Margaret of Anjou struggled for years to keep the English throne—for Henry VI.

Nor could a woman be sure of coming into her husband's property when he died. Inheritance laws varied widely from time to time and state to state—even from one city to another. A Roman law of the second century B.C. placed propertied women under male guardianship. That law was repealed in the next century. Christine de Pisan tried for years to get a court of law to award her the sizable sums of money that were owing to her dead husband. She failed, and turned to writing to support her family. In some parts of Europe, laws allowed a widow to be stripped of all property, including the dowry she herself had brought to the marriage. Other laws permitted a widow's father, brothers, or sons to force her to remarry against her will if they thought that a new marriage was the best way to preserve or increase the family's wealth.[25] Yet in other instances, the law was kinder to women. It was by inheritance that the tenth-century Aethelflaed became queen, for instance. Many of Europe's female merchants and guild members inherited their positions upon the death of a merchant or guildsman husband.

In most cases, however, when a widow did inherit property, she was expected to preserve it to hand on to her sons. Much as the lady of the manor acted as surrogate for her husband while he was away, widowed mothers acted as surrogates for their male offspring. After Margaret of Anjou's husband was captured by his enemies, she waged one last desperate—and doomed—battle on behalf of her son's right to inherit his father's crown. On the other

hand, women without sons were sometimes able to pass their property on to a daughter. Isabella of Spain left her crown to her daughter Juana. Alas for Isabella's good intentions. Juana, commonly
called "The Mad," proved incapable of ruling. She lost her throne
to her husband and, later, her son.

New Inequalities

By the early sixteenth century, as Isabella was making her ill-fated
plans for Juana, Europe was changing. Some changes were political. The rulers of Europe's many small kingdoms—Aragon and
Castile, for example—were joining into larger, more powerful,
nation-states like Spain. As that happened, Europe's patchwork of
local laws began to be replaced by unified national codes dictated
by the king and his lawmakers.

Other changes were social and economic. The so-called
Renaissance, a "rebirth" of interest in artistic and intellectual pursuits, began in Italy in the 1300s. By the sixteenth century, it had
spread throughout most of Europe. The Scientific Revolution of
the seventeenth and eighteenth centuries saw ancient beliefs and
superstitions beginning to give way to fresh new ideas about the
universe and how it works. Together, the Renaissance and the Scientific Revolution sparked a widespread enthusiasm for learning
and education. Last came the Industrial Revolution, which started
around 1750 and continued over the next century. The Industrial
Revolution was marked by the invention of the steam engine and
other complex machinery. It transformed Europe from a land of
open country dotted with small towns and farming villages into a
continent crowded with bustling cities, noisy factories—and thousands of new jobs.

The changes that began with the Renaissance and the appearance of the first nation-states opened vast new horizons for European men. Men had better chances for an education and more job
opportunities. As national governments edged toward democracy,

men also began winning greater political power than ever before. For women, by contrast, the changes meant narrower horizons and tighter restrictions.[26]

Why did the changes affect men and women so differently? A large part of the answer centers on men's age-old attitudes toward women. Not even the men who came up with the bold new ideas that marked the Renaissance and the Scientific Revolution could shake off those attitudes. Women were inferior to men, less capable, and less intelligent. That was an unquestionable fact of nature. So why should it even occur to these men to offer women anything but the most elementary education? Why would they think of admitting them to Europe's growing number of colleges and universities? Why allow them to become doctors or lawyers? Women did not have the ability to do that sort of "men's work." A woman's place was in the home, and it was her job to make that home comfortable for her husband and to care for his children. "All [a woman] has to do in this World is contained within the Duties of a Daughter, a Sister, a Wife, and a Mother," one Englishman wrote in 1712.[27]

Another reason that the changes that began with the Renaissance were so damaging to women had to do with the new national codes of law that were beginning to go into effect. Those law codes turned traditional negative attitudes toward women into legal fact. In the past, Europe's patchwork of law and custom had sometimes worked to protect women. But the new codes were locking them solidly into a position of legal inferiority. The 1563 English law that set the wages of female farmworkers at a fraction of those of male workers demonstrates how this happened. Before that measure became law, a woman might manage to negotiate a higher wage for herself. Now, it was illegal for her even to try.

Women were forced to accept other restrictions as well. According to the French legal code adopted in 1804 and widely copied in continental Europe, "the wife owes obedience to her husband." The husband was "head" of the household. He had the sole power to decide where the family would live. His wife had to get his explicit permission to inherit property, to work, to spend money or give it away, or to appear as a witness in a court case. A husband could forbid his wife to open a bank account. He could intercept her mail and read it over her objections.[28] Other laws, as we have seen, forbade women to seek an education or attempt to make a living as a professional. Nor did women have much hope of changing such restrictive measures. Even as more and more European men were winning the right to vote and hold public office, they were drawing up laws aimed at preventing women from doing either. Women were frozen out of government decision-making. "The early nineteenth century," Anderson and Zinsser write, "marked the nadir"—the low point—"of European women's options and possibilities."[29]

So what was life like for these women? For married women of the middle and upper classes, it was probably pleasant enough. Their chief complaint, in fact, may have been boredom. These women had husbands able to support them comfortably, while maids and other servants did the heavy housework and helped care for the children. But forbidden to work outside the home—or even to venture far from it on their own—kept from participating in public life, poorly educated and discouraged from intellectual pursuits, how were these women to occupy themselves? With "fancywork"—drawing, embroidery, and the like. A hint of how desperate some women must have been for novel ways to pass the time can be found in an 1850 list of "Elegant Arts for Ladies." Among the suggested arts: "the making of Feather Flowers, Hair Ornaments, Flowers or Fruit in Wax, Shell Work, Porcupine Quill Work, the gilding of Plaster Casts, Bead and Bugle Work, and Seaweed Pictures."[30]

Gilding plaster casts or constructing seaweed pictures may have been fine for the well-to-do, but very few nineteenth-century European women had time for such pursuits. The vast majority were out working, often in factories or as domestic servants.

Job openings for domestic servants multiplied in the nineteenth century as nations prospered and more families could afford to hire household help. Female servants were especially popular. By 1901 almost 83 percent of French servants were women. In England more than nine out of ten were female.

Girls and women in service had few rights. No limits were placed on their working hours, and there were no guarantees of time off. They could be beaten by their employers and fired at will. Their wages were small, particularly compared with those of male servants. A uniformed footman in an English household, "whose most laborious task is to wait at table," as an observer noted in 1798, earned at least £50 a year. A cook-maid got less than £20, although she "is mistress of her profession" and her job "requires a much greater degree of skill."[31]

For women in factories, wages were similarly low and the work as hard. One woman described her job as a youthful spinner in a German textile factory of the 1870s: "Spinning was a terrible torture. . . . We crouched hour after hour on the low stool behind the spinning wheel at the horrible monotonous and exhausting work, just spinning, spinning, spinning." Such torturous work was generally assigned to women and girls. One English factory inspector explained why. "Females," he told a government committee in 1844, " . . . are more easily induced to undergo severe bodily fatigue than men." Male laborers were trained to do less tiresome, more skilled jobs or were promoted to the rank of overseer or manager. As always, girls and women in spinning mills and other factories earned less than men. "A man thinks himself badly off if he cannot earn more than seventeen shillings a week," reported a union of working women in Manchester, England, in 1903. "There are thousands of girls in Manchester who think themselves lucky if they bring home seven shillings at the weekend. . . . These are . . . the wages of the poorest poor."[32]

Low pay, hard labor, unfair working conditions—such was the lot of poor women as the twentieth century dawned in Europe. A rigidly enforced uselessness outside the home, and the boredom that probably went with it, characterized the lives of middle- and upper-class women. Domestic and economic subservience to a father, brother, husband, or son, combined with a total lack of political power, were common to women of all classes across the continent.

Was it any different for the women of the New World?

3

WOMEN IN THE NEW WORLD

Margaret Hardenbroeck arrived, alone, in America in 1659. Margaret came from a prosperous trading family in the Netherlands, and was well-versed in business skills. She settled in the Dutch colony of New Amsterdam. Soon she was in trade herself, swapping pins, cooking oil, and vinegar for the beaver pelts and other furs that were in such demand back in Europe.

It wasn't long before Margaret married a fellow trader named Pieter Rudolphus DeVries. The DeVrieses maintained their own separate businesses, Pieter dealing in lumber, bricks, paper, tobacco, and other products. They had a daughter, Maria. When Pieter died in 1661, Margaret and Maria inherited everything that had been his.

Within two years Margaret had married again, this time to Frederick Philipsen. Now if New Amsterdam had been an English colony, governed under English law, this new marriage would have required Margaret to give up her first husband's property. But since New Amsterdam belonged to the Netherlands, Margaret was able to keep Pieter's estate. Dutch laws, unlike those of most other European countries, allowed a woman to inherit from her husband. Dutch women could also own businesses, buy and sell land, and sue in court for the repayment of debts.

So Margaret kept on trading. She also bought real estate in what is now New Jersey. As Frederick's full partner, she built up a profitable transatlantic shipping company.

Then, in August 1664, four English ships sailed into the harbor at New Amsterdam. The ships blockaded the harbor so that no Dutch vessels could enter it. New Amsterdam authorities held out for a month before surrendering. Margaret and Frederick found themselves living in the English colony of New York.

Old Ways in a New World

The change in the colony's ownership had little effect on Frederick. He dropped the "n" from his last name to make it sound more English, entered local government, and went on doing business as usual. Margaret did not. English law prevented her from continuing to act as her husband's business equal. Even when she wanted to buy more land, she had to ask Frederick to do it for her. The restrictions of England's male-dominated legal system left Margaret little opportunity to conduct business on her own.[1]

Margaret Hardenbroeck was just one of scores of New Amsterdam women who lost their financial independence under English rule. In the early 1660s there were 134 female traders in New Amsterdam and another forty-six in the upstate town of Albany. Ten years later, only forty-three women were actively trading in New York City. By 1700 there were no women traders at all in Albany. The female owners of breweries, laundries, and bakeshops had all but disappeared.[2]

Women in the former Dutch colony were not the only ones whose skills and abilities were ignored as colonization continued in the New World. When Europeans began exploring the Americas in the fifteenth and sixteenth centuries, they encountered the people they called "Indians." These Native Americans were divided into numerous tribes, each with its distinctive language, religion, and culture. Most Europeans, though, thought of them as a single group.

The various North American tribes did have some things in common. Most were hunter-gatherers. Like members of other hunter-gatherer societies, past and present, men and women shared the task of providing food. As a rule, men did the hunting, while women farmed.

Here is where the differences among the tribes become apparent. For some, hunting was more important than for others. In the land that came to be called Canada, for instance, winters are frigid and summers cool. The short growing season made meat essential to the diet. Hunters—men—were therefore the chief providers of food. Women deferred to them accordingly.[3]

For tribes living farther south, the situation was different. There, farming was at least as important as hunting, and the women who minded the fields could claim a good measure of independence and authority. Among the tribes of southern New England, women produced 90 percent of the calories consumed. In New York, Iroquois women harvested their crops, prepared them for eating, and stored them in large underground silos. When Iroquois men needed food—to carry with them on the warpath, perhaps—they had to get it from the women.

The women could, if they wished, refuse to give it to them. If the men were planning an attack that the women considered unwise, they would simply withhold the food the men needed. No food—no war.[4] Iroquois women could also refuse to feed a man whose behavior they deemed "undesirable." They could even deny him shelter in the great "longhouses" in which each extended family lived.[5] Iroquois women were not allowed to attend meetings of the Council of Elders, the tribe's highest governing body. They could, however, use their influence within the tribe to appoint a man to speak for them there.[6]

Few Europeans had any notion of the inner workings of Iroquois culture. Not until the 1840s, when the American Lewis Henry Morgan became the first anthropologist to make a systematic study of Native American lifestyles, did white people begin to understand the importance of women in tribal decision-making. Morgan was particularly impressed to observe that women had a far higher status in Iroquois society than they did in his own.[7] A century or two earlier, though, most Europeans simply failed to understand why "Indians" would allow women to do what they saw as men's work—farming. The fact that the Native Americans did allow it is one reason that so many Europeans and American colonists described them as "uncivilized" and "savages."

Colonists similarly failed to recognize the traditional importance of women among another segment of New World society, its black slaves. The first blacks were brought to Jamestown, Virginia, in 1619 and sold into servitude. By the end of the century, however, most Americans of African descent were not servants, but slaves. They were regarded as property, much like a house, or land, or livestock. When the Revolutionary War began in 1775, one of every six Americans was an African-American slave. Although a few slaves belonged to wealthy Boston, New York, and Philadelphia families, the majority were the property of farmers and plantation owners from Maryland to Georgia.[8]

At first, slave-owners relied mainly on male slaves to work their fields. But as time went by and the demand for farmworkers grew in the American South, slave-owners forgot their scruples about using women as farmers. By 1650 male and female slaves were hoeing corn and tobacco together. Soon small farms began turning into large plantations with acres of wheat and rye fields, lumber mills, fisheries, and craft shops where blacksmiths and other artisans plied their trades.

Along with establishing their plantations, slave-owners introduced a new division of labor based on gender. As in the mills and factories that were beginning to dot the European countryside, slave women tended to be assigned to the harder, more menial, jobs. "While men plowed and mastered crafts," Carol Berkin says, "women remained in the fields, left to hoe by hand what the plows could not reach. . . . When new tasks were added to women's work repertoire, they proved to be the least desirable: building fences, grubbing [clearing] swamps in the winter, cleaning seed out of winnowed grain, breaking new ground too rough for the plow, cleaning stables, and spreading manure." In the rice paddies of Georgia and the Carolinas, male slaves tended the plants, while women pounded the grain with mortars and pestles. The latter job was more grueling—and deadlier. Women slaves on the rice plantations died off faster than men.[9]

As slaves in America, African women had no hope of maintaining the status they had enjoyed in their homelands. Slave traders operated throughout West Africa, and the human cargoes they shipped to America rarely shared a language, a religion, or a similar cultural outlook. In America, slaves learned English—and lost their mother tongues. They adopted Christianity—and forgot the old gods and myths. They absorbed European and American attitudes about men and women and each one's "natural" place in the world. Like Margaret Hardenbroeck, like the women of the Iroquois and other Native American tribes, African-American women saw their value *as women* plummet as they came under the sway of Western European law and tradition.

In much of colonized North America, "Western European" meant "English." By 1770, England had laid claim to all the lands from Labrador and Newfoundland in the north to Georgia in the south, and from the Atlantic Ocean west across the Great Lakes. Throughout this area, English law and English customs prevailed. Even after the new United States won independence from England in 1783, its laws continued to be based on the English model. The same thing happened in Canada after that country became self-governing in 1867.

Nineteenth-Century American Women

For a nineteenth-century North American woman, how she lived her life depended in large part on where she lived. In farming communities, men did the plowing and planting, cared for the large livestock, hunted and fished, and handled the finances. Women cooked and cleaned, sewed and mended, and looked after their children. At the same time they contributed to the family income in all the traditional ways: tending gardens and marketing produce, raising chickens and other small livestock, selling eggs, butter, and cheese, and so on. If life on the farm became too hard, a man might decide to move West in search of a fresh start. Often, his wife and children went with him, traveling on foot or in a covered wagon. "Keeping house" on a mountain trail or within the boxlike confines of a farm wagon cannot have been easy, but thousands of pioneer women did it. At the same time, they did such outside jobs as gathering fuel, carrying water, and foraging for food.

For city women, life was different. Married women did all the usual household chores, as well as the shopping for food and other goods that nonfarm families could not produce for themselves. Penniless unmarried women and widows faced less certain futures. Some supported themselves by sewing or doing other forms of "piecework" in their own homes. Many went into domestic service in other people's houses, receiving the same low wages for doing the same heavy work as their European counterparts. But American women increasingly turned to the factory to support themselves.

Working conditions were as brutal in American factories as in European ones, and the hours as long. Workers at some New England mills were forced to stand at their machines for sixteen hours a day. In one Lynn, Massachusetts, shoe factory, men were paid just $3 for a week of sixteen-hour days. Women who worked the same hours earned $1. That was in 1859. The next year, workers in the Lynn factory went out on strike on March 7, demanding higher wages. Their employers refused even to discuss the matter. Workers marched through the city streets in a late-winter blizzard. The women carried signs proclaiming, "We Dare Battle for the Right, Shoulder to Shoulder with our Fathers, Husbands and Brothers." Six thousand marched—then, a few days later, ten thousand. Sympathetic workers throughout Massachusetts, Maine, and New Hampshire walked off their jobs as well. Finally, in April, factory owners gave in. Wages rose.[10]

Not all American women faced such a struggle in their daily lives. Those of the middle and upper classes sat in their genteel parlors, supervising their children while doing fancywork, just like their European sisters. They also devoted a good deal of time to light housekeeping, especially as families acquired the new luxury goods beginning to flood into the nation's shops. Women spent hours polishing silver, washing china, waxing furniture, and dusting knickknacks—or overseeing the slaves and servants who did the actual work for them. The ideal of the genteel woman's lifestyle is summed up in the Mother Goose marriage proposal:

"Curly-locks, Curly-locks, wilt thou be mine?
Thou shalt not wash the dishes, nor yet feed the swine;
But sit on a cushion, and sew a fine seam,
And feed upon strawberries, sugar, and cream."

Another rhyme is quite clear about how differently ladies and the men who provided for them were expected to live their lives . . .

"The king was in his counting-house,
Counting out his money;
The queen was in the parlor,
Eating bread and honey."

. . . as well as poking fun at the lowly female domestic servant:

"The maid was in the garden,
Hanging out the clothes;

When down came a blackbird
And pecked off her nose."

The maid in the garden, the slave with a hoe, the wife in her parlor, the millhand at her machine, the ever-busy farmwoman, the westward-bound pioneer, and the "savage" Native American—all were subservient to the white male population. Each seemed bound forever to her place in life. Then the women's-rights movement began.

Women's Rights

By some reckonings, the American women's-rights movement got under way with a convention organized by Elizabeth Cady Stanton and Lucretia Mott and held in July 1848, at Seneca Falls, New York. The men and women who gathered there issued a declaration stating that all people—not just all men—are created equal. They called for women to be educated about the laws of the land, to have the right to vote in state and federal elections, and to be allowed to speak in public without being silenced by their male relatives or colleagues.

Yet as important a milestone as the 1848 convention was, it did not represent the first step in the drive for women's rights. Stanton and Mott had earlier persuaded the New York state legislature to pass a law permitting married women there to control their own property.[11] As far back as 1821, a woman named Emma Willard had founded the first American college-level school for women, also in New York.[12] Today the Emma Willard School in Troy is a girls' college preparatory school.

Furthermore, women had already begun speaking out on issues they cared deeply about. Some who opposed slavery, for instance, wrote articles and organized meetings to call public attention to the cruel injustices of that system. By 1861 debate over the slavery question had escalated into war between the Northern states, which generally opposed the institution, and the Southern states, which supported it. The War Between the States—the Civil War—ended in 1865 with freedom for the nation's slave population.

If the meeting at Seneca Falls was not the first step in the women's-rights movement, neither was it the last. The meeting itself produced few immediate results. It would take two decades before Utah and Wyoming became the first states to grant women "partial suffrage." Partial suffrage enabled women to vote in state, county, and municipal elections.[13] By the late 1880s, most other states had followed the example of Utah and Wyoming.[14] But even then, opposition to full female suffrage remained strong. Decades after the 1848 convention, former U.S. president Grover Cleveland expressed his views on the matter. "Sensible and responsible women do not want to vote," Cleveland wrote in the magazine *Ladies' Home Journal*. "The relative positions to be assumed by man and woman in the working out of our civilization were assigned long ago by a higher intelligence."[15]

Sensible and responsible or not, women continued to press for change. Finally, in August 1920, the U.S. Constitution was amended to give all U.S. women the vote. (The Constitution is the document that outlines the structure and workings of the federal government.) It had taken American women seventy-two years and one month to win the same voting rights that men had enjoyed since the nation's founding.

And what about the 1848 declaration that all "people" are created equal? That idea has not yet been accepted in the United States. In 1923 a bill to amend the Constitution to ensure equal rights for women was introduced in Congress.[16] Not until 1972 did Congress approve the measure. "Equality . . . ," the proposed amendment read, "shall not be denied or abridged . . . on account of sex." The states, however, failed to ratify (agree to) the Equal Rights Amendment (ERA). To this day, U.S. women have no constitutional guarantee that they will receive equal treatment under the law.

War, Depression, War

Actually, women might not even have achieved full suffrage—or not as soon as they did—had it not been for a global calamity: World War I. That conflict began in Europe in 1914. In April 1917 the United States entered the war on the side of Britain, France, Russia, and Japan, who were already engaged in battle with Germany.

The war ended in 1918 with a victory for the United States, Britain, and their allies. By that time, two million American soldiers had been dispatched to Europe. More than half saw action. About 49,000 Americans were killed in battle, while another 57,000 died of disease.[17]

Some of the war dead were women. As always in wartime, women found a place for themselves on the front lines—or close behind them. Some performed such traditional tasks as nursing or organizing canteens where weary soldiers could find food and warmth. Others volunteered for the new duties of modern warfare, driving ambulances and relaying radio messages. Above all, women contributed to the war effort on the home front, abandoning their ordinary pursuits to replace the working men who had been called away to fight. All across Europe and America, women manufactured guns and ammunition, stitched uniforms, boots, and blankets, and worked the land to provide food for fighting men and citizens back home.

Most men were genuinely surprised by the women's determination and productivity. Convinced as they were that women's intelligence, skills, and abilities were far inferior to their own, men were astonished to see that women were every bit as capable as they were themselves. To their credit, many men transformed their astonishment into active support for the cause of women's suffrage. The British prime minister, Herbert Asquith, was among them. After learning that an English nurse serving in Belgium had been executed by the Germans, Asquith paid tribute to her—and to all the other women who were risking their lives for victory. "There are thousands of such women," he declared, "but a year ago we did not know it." Asquith, who had previously opposed giving women the vote, now favored doing so. It was the same for men in a number of other warring nations.[18] By the late 1920s, women's suffrage was the rule in America and much of Europe.

World War I altered women's lives in other ways. Some of the most "shocking" changes, say Bonnie Anderson and Judith Zinsser, had to do with their appearance. When the war began, women were dressing, as they had throughout the nineteenth century, in tight corsets reinforced with bone or steel and topped with heavy, long-sleeved bodices and layers of petticoats and skirts. The skirts covered their ankles, in a fashion that went back to the 1200s. Women also wore their hair long, often down to their knees or beyond.[19]

All that had to change as women turned to driving ambulances and assembling munitions. Long hair and long skirts had always endangered female factory workers. Either was apt to become entangled in fast-moving machinery. In the past, though, women had simply been told to be careful. Some were fined or punished in other ways when an accident did occur.[20] The obvious solution—women cutting their hair and shortening their skirts—was unthinkable. The nineteenth-century laws of such European countries as France and Germany expressly forbade women to dress like men.[21] But in 1914, with women's work central to the war effort, attitudes had to change. Hemlines were already rising by December of that year, and in the next winter they were a full 10 inches (25 centimeters) off the ground. Corsets disappeared. In the 1920s women began wearing slacks in public. Thousands "bobbed" their hair into short, sleek styles.[22]

Many of the new freedoms that women won during and after World War I turned out to be permanent. They never did resume wearing corsets, for example. Those who had won the vote kept it. Other freedoms, however, such as the freedom of well-to-do women to work outside the home, were quickly snatched away. Once the fighting was over, former soldiers of all nations lined up in the workplace, demanding their old jobs back. Women were asked—or ordered—to step aside. In some countries, they received bonuses to hand their jobs over to men. In others, they were simply fired. Those with husbands found it especially difficult to keep a job.[23] Remember what happened to Maine kindergarten teacher Madeline Hennessey when she got married in 1937.

By the 1930s, however, still more changes had come into women's lives. This was the decade of the Great Depression, the economic catastrophe that struck not only the United States and Canada, but throughout the industrialized world. During the Depression, thousands of banks and businesses failed. Millions of people lost their jobs. By 1933 nearly one-fourth of the largely male U.S. workforce was unemployed. As usual in time of crisis, women assumed added responsibilities. They signed up for whatever full-, part-time, or temporary jobs they could find. Some took in boarders or sold goods door-to-door. Many opened their homes to relatives even worse-off than they were or organized relief efforts to help the most desperately poor.

The Depression dragged on throughout the 1930s. It ended— but not before a new global calamity was brewing. This was World War II, which began in Europe in 1939. Canada joined in the fighting at once, and the United States did likewise in 1941. Before the war ended with another Allied victory in 1945, soldiers from both countries had seen combat on three continents—Europe, Asia, and Africa.

Once again, women went to war along with men. This time, however, they moved beyond their customary roles as volunteers to become official members of the armed forces. In May 1942 the U.S. Women's Auxiliary Army Corps (later the Women's Army Corps, or WAC) was established. Two months later, Congress voted to create a Women's Reserve of the United States Naval Reserve (WAVES).[24] WACs and WAVES served in communications centers and as secretaries, nurses, and the like. They did not go into combat. Three years after the war ended, Congress expressly banned women from taking part in active fighting.[25]

On the home front, women threw themselves into wartime production as wholeheartedly as they had a generation earlier. In the United States the female factory worker was personified as "Rosie the Riveter." Posters advertising the nation's defense industries depicted "Rosie" as a young woman in overalls, her hair covered with a bandanna, flexing a muscle.

That Rosie was only a symbol. But there was a real-life Rosie as well. She was Rose Will Monroe, a riveter in an aircraft factory in Ypsilanti, Michigan. Rose Monroe was persuaded to appear in a short film made to raise money for the war effort by encouraging the public to buy war bonds and stamps. She must have been convincing. Americans spent more than $156 billion for the cause.[26]

Rose Monroe died in 1997. In an obituary, *The New York Times* noted that she had taken her riveting job both out of patriotism, "to fulfill a call to arms" and out of need, as a widow with young children to support. After the war, Rose went right on working. She drove a cab, ran a beauty parlor, and headed up her own home construction company.[27]

In continuing to work, Rose Monroe was unusual. After 1945 most American women dropped out of the workforce, once more surrendering their well-paid factory jobs to returning soldiers. Women retreated to their parlors, devoting themselves to domesticity and—as perhaps never before—motherhood. The nation's birthrate rose 50 percent between 1945 and 1955, in what came to be known as the "baby boom" years. "Most women," says one historian, seemed "willing to accept motherhood as their highest ambition."[28]

But not for long.

4

HOMEMAKERS AND CAREERWOMEN

The birthrate wasn't the only thing booming in the United States in the years after World War II. The economy was, as one expert put it, in a "take-off" mode.[1]

American factories had not produced many consumer goods during the war. Rosie the Riveter and her friends on the production line had had their hands full turning out war supplies. Now, with the war over, the federal government saw to it that factories got all the assistance they needed in switching back to peacetime production. Returning soldiers came home to find plenty of jobs—good, secure, high-paying jobs—waiting for them. They also found a federal government eager to reward them for their service by helping them pay for college or vocational training, buy a house, or start a business of their own.[2]

Millions took advantage of the opportunity. They got jobs, signed up for school, married, purchased homes, and began doing their part to fuel the baby boom. At the same time, they embarked on a spending spree, snapping up diapers and bicycles, dishwashers and vacuum cleaners and tennis racquets, automobiles and golf clubs, and all the other toys and necessities that had been scarce during the war years.

The spending had the nation's factories humming, barely able to keep pace with the demand. New factories were built. Airports expanded to accommodate growing fleets of freight and passenger planes. Housing developments, their streets lined with rows of ranch-style dwellings, appeared across the country. New developments—whole new neighborhoods—blossomed in what, just weeks before, had been open fields and farmland. Schools were built, and classrooms added on, as more and more baby-boom children reached kindergarten age. Churches and synagogues got additions, as well. Office buildings sprang up. The first shopping malls materialized. Suburbs mushroomed as Americans moved out from the city and in from the farm. To connect one suburb to another—and all of them to the malls and workplaces—the federal government undertook to construct a huge interstate highway system. That, and the other new building projects, meant thousands more jobs, which in turn meant increased spending on goods and services. Altogether, in the brief period between 1950 and 1965, the U.S. economy produced as much as it had in all the years from 1607 to 1950. From 1965 to 1980, the nation's wealth doubled again.[3]

The booming economy made Americans richer. That is, it made most white Americans richer. Blacks, Native Americans, and members of other racial minorities were largely left out of the postwar boom.

At the same time, the new prosperity drastically altered the way suburbanites lived and worked together as families. For the first time in history, a nation was wealthy enough to enable the majority of its adult female population to live the kind of stay-at-home lifestyle formerly reserved for the privileged few.

45

Homemakers

As depicted in the media—books, magazines, television, the movies—the American wife and mother of the 1940s, 50s, and 60s was a happy woman. Advertisements from those years show her, smiling and perfectly groomed, wearing a tidy outfit (called a "housedress") protected by a ruffled apron, demonstrating the use of some household appliance—a washing machine, perhaps, or a vacuum cleaner. Typically, she wears pearl beads and high-heeled shoes. Her appearance suggests glamour and luxury, not heavy housework. This woman is a "homemaker," the mid-twentieth-century version of the queen in her parlor.

Was the depiction accurate? The average American woman of the era definitely enjoyed a degree of luxury undreamed of by earlier generations. She had plenty to eat. She lived in a comfortable home filled with labor-saving gadgets. No rules kept her from attending school or college. She had the right to vote. And, unlike nearly all other women before her, she had no need to contribute to the household income. Not for her the exhaustion of factory work or the bother of producing and peddling handicrafts or food items. She was free to devote herself full-time to caring for her home and playing with her children. After all, she had a husband to go out into the world and earn the money that supported her and her family. Even if a couple divorced—and that rarely happened in the late 1940s and 50s—the man continued to provide his former wife with financial support (alimony) until she remarried. This was a far cry indeed from the time, five or six centuries earlier, when a women might be forced to surrender her own dowry when her husband died!

Yet looked at in another way, there was an aspect to the lives of those long-ago women that the postwar homemaker might have envied. As we saw in chapter 2, European women before the time of the Renaissance were not just wives and mothers but active participants in the world at large. Although most married and had children, that didn't stop them from also working in construction, setting up as merchants, acting as courtiers, going into combat, joining craft guilds, prescribing for the sick, and so forth. And they were paid for their work. They weren't paid as much as men were, and they might not get to keep what they did earn. But at least they had the satisfaction of knowing that they had an important place, not only within the family but also as members of the larger human society around them. Few women in mid-twentieth-century America could feel such satisfaction. Most focused their energies on their domestic role. Most seemed content to find their greatest satisfaction in the accomplishments of their husbands and children.

And how did the life of the new American homemaker compare with that of the genteel woman of the nineteenth century? Earlier ladies may have been bored stiff in their comfortable parlors, reduced as they were to creating useless ornaments out of seaweed and porcupine quills. But at least they did have plenty of genuine leisure, with servants—or slaves—to do the cooking and cleaning and help with child care.

Baby-boom era wives and mothers had little if any domestic help. The postwar economy was so robust that few white girls and young women needed to hire themselves out as cooks and nursemaids. As a result, most homemakers were left to fend for themselves. Besides running the washing machine and ferrying a vacuum cleaner from room to room in pearls and high heels, a wife and mother was expected to bake cookies with her children and serve her husband a gourmet dinner each evening. She had to do the ironing (permanent press was not yet on the market, and even sheets and pillowcases were customarily ironed in those days), pack school lunches, mop floors, scrub the toilet, sew on buttons, de-flea the dog, weed the flower garden, and do the dozens of other jobs that had become part of managing a modern American household. She probably also volunteered at a local hospital or in her children's schools and served as den mother for a pack of Cub Scouts, as well as driving in car pools, shopping, picking up clothes at the dry cleaner, and running the family's other errands. In fact, she must have felt less like the queen—sitting in the parlor, eating bread and honey—than like the maid—hanging out the clothes and doing everything else around the house, sixteen hours a day, seven days a week. Unlike the underpaid maid, however, the homemaker received no salary at all for what she did.

Of course she didn't. People are paid for working, and homemaking wasn't considered "work." Work was a career or profession. It was performed in a place of business, a factory, an office, a store. Work was something men did so that women could afford to stay at home.

Which is exactly where most of them were when some began asking, "Is this all there is to life?"

The "Feminine Mystique"?

One of the women asking herself that question was Betty Friedan. Like many others of her generation, Betty Friedan liked school and went on to graduate from Smith College in 1942. For a while, she worked as a reporter. Then she married, had children, and stopped working. In 1957 Friedan was a full-time homemaker in suburban New York. She was as busy as any other wife and mother—but considerably less happy than advertisements and the media were telling her she should be.[4]

Was she the only unhappy homemaker in America? Friedan drew up a questionnaire and sent it to two hundred of her former college classmates. Their responses convinced her that she was not alone. Many of those women, and others she interviewed over the next several years, expressed strong feelings of "dissatisfaction" and a "yearning" for a more challenging way of life. In 1963 Friedan published her findings in a book called *The Feminine Mystique*.

The Feminine Mystique created a sensation. Friedan had chosen the title as a way of summing up society's message to postwar women: that "truly feminine women do not want careers, higher education, [or] political rights." Women should leave such matters to men. *Their* purpose in life "was to seek fulfillment as wives and mothers."[5]

From page one, Friedan made it plain that she could not accept the idea of such a mystique. She did not believe that it was possible to make broad distinctions between people's talents, abilities, and aspirations based solely upon which sex they happened to be. Friedan was a "feminist," one who takes it for granted that a woman should be as free as a man to live up to her full potential as a human being.

Not everyone agreed with all of Betty Friedan's conclusions, but most who read her book were jolted into a new awareness of the inequality between the sexes. Decades earlier, women had thought that winning the right to vote would make them equal with men. But it had not. Being able to vote wasn't the same as being part of government, and there were almost no women in government in the 1950s. Nor were there many women in business or the professions. The unmarried women and older married women who did seek paid employment were steered in the direction of becoming secretaries, nurses, and grade-school teachers. Very few were executives, doctors, or high-school principals. In terms of education, Friedan pointed out, women had actually lost ground during the century. In 1920 there were forty-seven women in U.S. colleges for every one hundred men. In 1958 there were only thirty-five college women for every hundred men. Of those women who did enroll in college, 60 percent left before graduating, either to marry or because they feared that having too much education would make it difficult for them to find husbands.[6]

Girls dropping out of school because they were afraid of not getting married? Intelligent women kept fully occupied with housework and child care, or shunted into jobs that required them always to take orders from men? More than half of the country's total population virtually unrepresented in government? Women routinely being *told*—not *asked*—what they wanted out of life? The women's movement, dormant since women had won the vote in 1920, burst into new life.

The New Feminism

Twenty years after *The Feminine Mystique* first hit the shelves, Betty Friedan wrote a new introduction to the book. In it she marveled at women's advances since 1963. "Firewomen, chairpersons . . . take-out food . . . women rabbis, women prime ministers . . . women's studies . . . more women now going to college than men . . . the two-paycheck family . . . Who could have predicted some of these? Not I, certainly."[7]

Perhaps Friedan couldn't have predicted the changes, but she had done her part to help bring them about. Three years after publishing her book, she and others founded the National Organization for Women (NOW). One of NOW's goals—not yet achieved—was persuading Congress and the states to adopt the Equal Rights Amendment. Other goals included getting new federal laws to ensure equal educational opportunities for women, to guarantee equal pay for men and women doing the same jobs, and to offer better child care to working mothers. NOW's membership is about 250,000 women and men.

Also helping to advance the new feminist cause was a federal civil-rights law that Congress passed in 1964. That measure was originally intended to ensure black Americans their full rights as U.S. citizens.

Even though slavery had ended a century before, state and local laws denied most black children a good education. Other laws kept blacks from using such public facilities as restrooms and drinking fountains and from exercising their right to vote. Such discrimination—unfair treatment—based on race was common around the country, but it was legally enforced most strongly in the Southern states. Not surprisingly, when the civil-rights bill was introduced in Congress, much of the opposition to it came from Southern senators and representatives.

In an odd twist of fate, that is how women happened to be included under the provisions of the bill. Hoping to make the proposed law look so ridiculous that Congress would turn it down, a senator from Virginia added the word "sex" to its language. Along with forbidding discrimination based on race, color, religion, and national origin, the bill, if passed, would outlaw discrimination based on sex. The bill did pass. Thanks to a senator's "joke," American women had scored a major victory.[8]

Their fight for equality, however, was far from over. The Civil Rights Act of 1964 was law. Under it, a federal Equal Employment Opportunities Commission (EEOC) was set up. The EEOC's task was to ensure an end to any form of on-the-job discrimination. Few federal officials, however, were eager to enforce the new law's provisions against sex discrimination. One administrator laughingly told reporters that all the law really meant was that men could now seek jobs as scantily clad cocktail waitresses. It was out of feminist anger at such remarks that NOW was born.[9] NOW took the Civil Rights Act seriously and intended to pressure the government into making sure that employers did, too.

One battle came over the issue of airplane stewardesses. In 1966 U.S. airline companies automatically fired any stewardess who married or reached the age of thirty. Most people assumed that the airlines' policy was aimed at luring male ticket-buyers with the promise of attractive young women to wait on them during the flight. Betty Friedan wasn't so sure. "I realized how much money the airlines saved by firing those pretty stewardesses before they had time to accumulate pay increases, vacation time, and pension rights," she wrote later.

Friedan and her fellow feminists vowed to put a halt to the airlines' age discrimination policies, and they did. Today, "stewardesses" no longer fly on the nation's airplanes. "Flight attendants" do. Many flight attendants are married and well over age

51

thirty. Many have children. Many are men. What is more, while men have joined women serving in the cabin, women have begun piloting commercial airline flights along with men.

Another early skirmish involved newspaper "Help Wanted" advertisements. Until the late 1960s, those ads were divided into two sections: "Help Wanted: Male" and "Help Wanted: Female." The former listed job openings for factory foremen, office managers, road-construction flaggers, snow-shovelers. And the latter? Secretaries, hair stylists, salesclerks, baby-sitters. Separating employment opportunities according to sex was one way females were steered toward low-paying, low-prestige positions. Under the Civil Rights Act of 1964, single-sex want ads were illegal, just as illegal as a want ad would be if it called for all job applicants to be white or Catholic or Mexican-American. Feminists demanded that the federal government order newspapers and other advertising media to stop running sex-segregated want ads. The federal government did. That gave girls and women the chance at least to apply for the better-paid jobs formerly set aside for boys and men.[10]

In fighting for what they were calling "Women's Liberation," feminists adopted a number of different tactics. Some of their protests were flippant, even deliberately outrageous. During the struggle over want ads, for instance, women dumped bundles of newspapers in the offices of the men charged with enforcing the Civil Rights Act of 1964. Others draped frilly aprons and mock typewriters over the fence outside the White House in Washington, D.C.[11] Still others tried to disrupt beauty pageants on the grounds that such contests are demeaning to women. Such tactics cast feminists in a negative light, and led some Americans to dismiss them scornfully as "Women's Libbers."[12]

Other protests were more traditional. In 1966 Betty Friedan testified in court against the airlines' policy of firing stewardesses. The judge listened. Women wrote letters, made phone calls, organized meetings, and lobbied members of Congress. And, on August 26, 1970, tens of thousands of them marched down New York

City's Fifth Avenue in what its organizers had billed as the Women's Strike for Equality.

August 1970 marked the fiftieth anniversary of the ratification of the Nineteenth Amendment to the U.S. Constitution. That amendment had given women the right to vote. Now, half a century later, women were calling for "the end of millenniums of oppression."[13]

At first, New York City police tried to keep the marchers—who included hundreds of men—confined to the sidewalks. It was impossible. The enthusiastic demonstrators overflowed into the broad avenue and no one even attempted to hold them back. "On August 26," Betty Friedan recalls, "it suddenly became both political and glamorous to be a feminist."[14]

Political, glamorous . . . and necessary. For the world of the 1970s was very different from the world of the 1940s and 50s. Women were no longer regarded as a special, leisured class of people. Changes had come into their lives that made it imperative for them to get out of the house, go to work, and earn on an equal basis with men.

As in earlier times, some of the changes were economic. The U.S. manufacturing industry had run into trouble. During the post-World War II boom years, most Americans had bought only American-made goods. Now they were buying cars and cameras made in Germany and Japan, clothing stitched in China, electrical appliances assembled in Taiwan, and shoes from Europe, Latin America, and the Far East. American production slowed, and thousands of workers lost their jobs.

Many of them managed to land new jobs. But these jobs were not like the well-paid jobs of the postwar baby boom years. Instead of filling positions in steel mills and on factory assembly lines, former industrial workers found themselves cleaning office buildings, delivering pizzas, and pumping gas. Such new "service sector" jobs did not pay well. Moreover, many offered only part-time or temporary employment.

Along with unemployment and lower wages came inflation—rising prices. The cost of goods and services soared throughout the 1970s.[15] Many families discovered that a husband's paycheck was no longer enough to cover household expenses. Increasingly, the pressure was on women to resume contributing to the family income.

Another factor pushing women back into the workplace during the 1970s was divorce. In the baby boom years, divorce was relatively rare. There were about 400,000 divorces in the United States in 1960. In 1976 there were 1.1 million, and in 1992 an all-time record 1.2 million marriages broke up. Even allowing for population increases between 1960 and 1992, the nation's divorce rate rose steadily during that time. Since 1992 it has dipped slightly.[16]

For most divorced women, the question is not, "Shall I get a job?" but "How fast can I get a job?" or "How fast can I get a better-paying job?" Studies show that in the years after a divorce, a man's personal financial situation improves. A woman's worsens. The difference is partly due to the fact that divorced men are no longer expected to pay alimony to their ex-wives. Divorced fathers are supposed to continue helping to support their children, but many fail to meet their obligations. When fathers don't pay their share, mothers have to take up the slack. Another reason that divorced men are generally economically better off than their ex-wives is that—even today—most women's wages are substantially less than most men's.[17] The feminist goal of equal pay for equal work assumed new importance as the divorce rate grew and single mothers became commonplace.

Back to the Workplace

Economic necessity, political happenstance, and the emergence of the new feminism combined to thrust women back into the workplace during the last quarter of the twentieth century. When 1976 began, just one woman had ever served in the U.S. Senate. Only two had been named to presidential Cabinet posts. No women had been appointed to the Supreme Court, the nation's highest court of law. Women had never been admitted to the U.S. Military Academy at West Point, or to any of the other federal service academies. No woman had been accepted into the U.S. astronaut program, headed up a college mathematics department, held a leadership position in any major religious group, anchored a television news program, or become a chief executive officer in a Fortune 500 company.

We saw in chapter 1 how different things are today. Jill Barad, CEO at the Mattel toy company, and Jamie Tarses of ABC-TV are examples of women who are making it to the top in the business world. Women not only anchor news programs, but they also report the news and *make* the news as members of Congress, the Cabinet, the Supreme Court, and as elected and appointed officials in the nation's statehouses, city halls, and town councils. The United States and Canada lag behind much of the rest of the world in female participation in government. But in both countries, such participation is greater now than ever in the past.

Women are also finding new acceptance in organized religion. The U.S. Episcopal Church ordained its first woman priest in 1976. Twenty years later, the church had 1,452 female priests—and six female bishops. Other denominations are ordaining women as well. In 1996 more than 2,300 women were serving as Baptist ministers, nearly 5,000 women as Methodist ministers, and 10 as Methodist bishops. Evangelical Lutherans, Presbyterians, Unitarian-Universalists, and members of the United Church of Christ had similarly welcomed female clergy. More than 300 women rabbis were serving Reform, Conservative, and Reconstructionist Jewish congregations.

Women have moved into scientific and technological fields, as well. Thirty years ago, few women even aspired to become doctors. In 1996 a woman became chairperson of the Board of Trustees of the American Medical Association.[18] The next year, the former director of Boston's Logan International Airport, a woman, was named to head the Federal Aviation Administration.[19] Female astronauts have walked in space.

Women are an increasing presence in the U.S. military. First admitted to the service academies in the fall of 1976, women now routinely graduate as officers. They no longer serve as members of sex-segregated units like the WACs or WAVES. Women today represent nearly 14 percent of personnel on active military duty.[20] Revised federal regulations allow them to pilot fighter planes and fly supply missions into combat zones.[21] In 1991 a female naval officer became the first woman to take command of a ship at sea.[22]

Female athletes are seeing new opportunities, too. When the first modern International Olympic Games were held in 1896, women were not allowed to compete in a single event. Nearly a century later, one-third of Olympic events were still men-only. Men played ice hockey, for instance. Women did not.[23] By the end of the 1990s, most Olympic sports were open to women. Ice hockey was one of them. Others included the 5,000-meter run, the triple jump, and softball. Two professional women's basketball leagues—the American Basketball League and the Women's National Basketball Association—played their first seasons in 1996 and 1997, respectively. Also in 1997, the men's National Basketball Association hired its first two female referees.[24]

Sports . . . the military . . . the sciences . . . religion . . . politics . . . business—these are only some of the fields in which women are carving out successful careers today. Like the women of pre-Renaissance Europe, like the Iroquois women who greeted white people in America, like West African women before they were seized and sold into slavery, modern working women have the satisfaction of knowing that they play an essential role outside the home as well as within its confines. That's the good news.

The bad news is that so many of these women claim that they still face a "glass ceiling" of discrimination in the workplace.

Do they?

5

GOOD NEWS—
AND BAD

Listen to Pam—who doesn't want her last name used—talk about the time she spent working for a large New York City consulting firm. Pam's first after-college job was at an advertising agency. She joined the consulting firm a couple of years later.

That firm was in the business of helping corporate executives deal with the public, especially during a crisis. For example, Pam says, after a deadly airplane accident, airline executives might hire the firm to figure out how best to present information about the crash and its probable cause to news reporters. The consultants might also suggest what people at the airline could do to help the victims' grieving families confront the tragedy.

It was not an enjoyable job, Pam says now. Oh, the work itself was interesting and challenging. The problem concerned the way she was treated by her bosses and co-workers—all but one of them male.

"There was no respect," Pam explained in a telephone

interview. "It was a sort of 'boys' club,' and I was the outsider. If I tried to say something—to make a suggestion or ask a question—I'd be patted on the back and told to scurry away. Or I'd get my head chopped off."

Would it have been different if she had been a man? "You bet it would!" Once, when Pam had stepped out of her office for a few minutes, her boss went through her files looking for some papers. "He didn't even need the papers until the next day," Pam said angrily. "He would never have dared search a guy's desk." After a little more than a year on the job, Pam quit. She planned to spend a few weeks traveling before returning to New York to think about her future.

Meet the Glass Ceiling

Had Pam run up against a glass ceiling in her consulting job? She certainly ran up against a lack of respect from her boss and fellow workers. That lack of respect had nothing to do with the kind of person Pam was. It had nothing to do with her qualifications for the job, or her ability to do the job to a client's satisfaction. It was based entirely on the fact that she was a woman.

Of course, Pam didn't have to resign just because she felt over-looked and underappreciated. She could have chosen to stay on in her job, battling for respect at every turn. But suppose she had done just that. Would she have won promotions at the same rate as her male coworkers? Would her salary have kept pace with theirs? It seems unlikely. Lack of respect based on a person's gender may not in itself constitute a glass ceiling. But it can be one pane in that invisible, yet solid, barrier that many women believe still keeps them from attaining their full potential as members of the nation's workforce.

Other women encounter other aspects of the glass ceiling. Some report outright hostility—even threats—from men on the job. Others mention the isolation they feel when they are the only women in the workplace. Others tell tales of sexual harassment, both verbal, in the form of crude or overly familiar language, and physical. Working mothers despair at the difficulty of balancing the conflicting demands of home and work. Women who are members of minority groups often come up against barricades based on race as well as sex. Women of all races complain that it is generally harder for them to rise in a business or profession than it would be if they were men—and that it gets harder and harder the further they do rise. Many complain about earning less money than men who are doing the same or similar work. Some claim to be unable to find any job at all in the career field of their choice.

Getting the Job

Let's begin by examining that last claim. Are women really kept out of some jobs simply because they are women? Sometimes it seems as if the answer must be no. In *The New Yorker* magazine of September 29, 1997, for instance, one writer speculated lightheartedly as to why there were no female doormen (doorwomen?) in New York City. Can't a woman "don a pair of white gloves . . . and push an elevator button?" he wondered. Don't women's eyes have the "upper-cornea strength" needed to spot oncoming taxicabs and hail them for waiting passengers? Apparently not.[1]

Then, not three months later, came this headline in *The New York Times*: "Opening Door, Plaza Hotel Makes Woman a Doorman." Sure enough, there was a photo of 31-year-old Sheila Connors, a former police officer and would-be actress. Jauntily decked out in a smart-looking cap, braided uniform, cab-hailing whistle, and—of course—white gloves, she stood proudly in front of one of New York City's best-known luxury hotels. True, Connors had the job only temporarily, during the holiday season. And true, she almost lost the position when one top hotel official began worrying about how guests might react to the sight of a woman summoning taxis and hefting luggage. Fearing she would see her job slip away before she had a chance to begin filling it, Connors telephoned news reporters. The resulting publicity left her securely on duty at the Plaza—at least until 1998 began.[2]

Sheila Connors isn't the only woman who has turned to the media, or used some other equally drastic tactic, to get or keep a job. Brenda Berkman was a lawyer in her thirties when she decided that what she really wanted to be was a New York City firefighter. That was back in the early 1980s, when fire departments were strictly male. New York City refused to admit her to its fire academy. So Berkman went to court, arguing that barring her from training as a firefighter was a form of sex discrimination. She won her case. In 1982 she and thirty-nine other women entered the academy. Today, women serve as firefighters in towns and cities around the country. Berkman herself has risen to the rank of lieutenant in Manhattan's Ladder Company 12.[3]

Other women have found their way into nontraditional jobs. Jane Perlov joined the New York City police department in 1981, one of the first women to do so. In 1997 she was promoted to chief of detectives for the New York City borough of Queens. The only woman ever named to such a high police post in the city, Perlov commands a force of more than 500 detectives, male and female.[4] Around the country, women work as prison guards, postal carriers, airline pilots and navigators, sports reporters and broadcasters, bus drivers and dispatchers, taxi drivers, construction workers, and in dozens of other jobs that, only a few years ago, were reserved for men.

Yet the picture for women isn't all rosy. In 1995 Jane Perlov was one of New York City's 5,618 female police officers. Those 5,618 women represented only fifteen percent of the city force, the usual cutoff figure for what is called a "token" number of the workforce.[5] A token is defined as a sign or symbol. So a city (or any other entity) that hires only a token number of employees who are women, or black, or who belong to some other category, is making a gesture that is more symbolic than anything else.

Tokenism in the workplace amounts to a policy of making an on-the-surface-only effort toward full integration.

Other northeast cities fail to achieve even tokenism in their police forces. Less than 11 percent of Niagara Falls, New York, police officers are women. In Hartford, Connecticut, the figure is 9 percent and in Cherry Hill, New Jersey, 5 percent. Female fire-fighters are a rare breed in New Jersey, as well. Of the state's 4,000 full-time firefighters in 1997, six were women.[6]

In New York City, the lone doorwoman was a token, as well. A sprinkling of women can be found throughout most of the work-force today. But the number of women actually making careers in nontraditional positions frequently remains at or below the token level.

Take jobs in the sciences, for example. More women than ever before are aiming for careers in science and engineering. As the 1990s began, women were earning 40 percent—close to half—of all U.S. undergraduate college science degrees. They were earning one-third of all master of science degrees and nearly a third of doc-toral degrees in scientific fields. At the same time, women gener-ally were performing better academically than their male classmates. In every field from business to the humanities and from education to the arts, women's undergraduate grades aver-aged 3.07, a high B, to men's 2.92, a low B.[7]

But in spite of their degrees and their grades, women scientists are less likely than male scientists to find good jobs after gradua-tion. Female scientists, says one researcher who has studied employment rates in the field, are anywhere from two to five times more likely to be jobless than male scientists.[8]

What is more, women are less likely than men to be selected for membership in a prestigious scientific or professional organi-zation. The U.S. National Academy of Science elected fifty-nine new members in 1992. Four were women.[9] These dismal statistics may be changing. After all, a woman did assume a top position in the American Medical Association in 1996. Yet even the most optimistic women agree that they remain seriously underrepresented in the science lab, just as they are in the fire station or police precinct house.

Or in government. It's true that there were a record nine women in the U.S. Senate in 1997—but there were *ninety-one* male Senators. Four out of fourteen U.S. cabinet officers were women— less than 30 percent of the total. As for the nation's statehouses, a minuscule one-twenty-fifth of U.S. governors were female in 1997.

It comes down to this: Despite the publicity that surrounds a Sheila Connors or a Jane Perlov, most women still find it hard to break out of their traditional job roles. The overwhelming majority of working women continue to be grouped in so-called female jobs. According to a survey conducted in the early 1990s, three-quarters of U.S. working women were employed in five categories: household worker; service employee (waitress, for example); elementary school teacher; nurse; and secretarial or clerical office worker.[10] These job categories are commonly described as "pink-collar ghettos." *Pink* because that color is more often associated with women's clothing than with men's. *Ghetto* refers to a setting (originally a section of a city) populated by members of a particular racial or religious group. So a pink-collar ghetto is an office, or day-care center, or nursing home, or any other workplace in which most of the employees are women.

Pink-collar ghettos show no sign of disappearing soon. In 1996 somewhat less than 7 million American men, age sixteen and older, were reported working in service occupations. That same year, more than 10 million women of similar ages had service jobs. In 1996 about 1.5 million men were teaching in the nation's elementary and high schools, and more that 3.5 million women were doing the same. In the health-care field, jobs were divided into two categories: health diagnosing occupations (doctors) and health assessment and treating occupations (nurses, lab technicians, and the like). The former employed 715,000 men and 245,000 women; the latter, 403,000 men and 2.4 million women.[11]

Even when women go into business for themselves, researchers find, they tend to stick to traditional work roles. Nearly 40 percent of all new U.S. businesses were being founded by women in the 1990s. But those businesses were more likely to be home-based beauty shops, day-care centers, and bakeries than construction firms or computer labs.[12]

Why? One reason may be that many women feel more comfortable working in a traditional field. Another is that a woman may not be able to persuade a bank or other financial institution to lend her the money to set up a nontraditional line of business. When Patty Abramson and two other women applied for a loan to start a public-relations firm, for instance, they were turned down. Bank officials were reluctant to lend money to the women directly for what the bankers considered to be a risky business undertaking. "Only if your husbands sign for the loan" will we invest in your venture, one bank officer told them. That was in the 1970s.

Abramson and the others eventually raised the funds they needed. Today, theirs is among the most successful public-relations enterprises in Washington, D.C. In 1997, hoping to make it easier for other women to start their own businesses, Abramson helped found the Women's Growth Capital Fund. The fund makes money available exclusively to female entrepreneurs—founders of new businesses. That's a step in the right direction, Abramson believes. But she notes that of the 1,200 new U.S. firms that received high-risk business loans in 1996, only thirty were owned by women. Of the $33 billion invested in high-risk ventures between 1991 and 1995, just 2 percent went to companies run by women.[13]

Even in fiction, it can be hard for working women to move beyond tradition. When Blondie, a character in the newspaper comic strip "Blondie," decided she wanted to take a job outside the home, she faced stubborn opposition from her husband, Dagwood. Blondie eventually gained Dagwood's approval of her new career—as a caterer.

What, in the end, is the answer to the question we asked earlier? Are some careers simply off-limits to women, even in token numbers?

A very few really are. As we saw in chapter 4, thousands of women currently serve as ministers in Protestant churches. About 300 have become Reform, Conservative, or Reconstructionist rabbis. In 1998 two Orthodox Jewish congregations in New York City took the unprecedented step of hiring one woman each to serve as an intern. Such internships have always been reserved for men on their way to the rabbinate. No Orthodox woman has ever become a rabbi. Is that about to change?[14]

One thing that seems definite is that no woman in any ultra-Orthodox Jewish sect will become a rabbi. Among these extra-traditional groups, women are not permitted to worship alongside their fathers, husbands, brothers, and sons, let alone act as their spiritual advisors. Equally off-limits to women is priesthood in the Roman Catholic Church. Despite calls from many American Catholics to ordain women, Pope John Paul II adamantly opposes the idea. Since becoming pope in 1978, John Paul has repeatedly stated that the subject of women priests is not even up for debate. The male priesthood is "willed by the Lord," he maintains.[15] However, women now may be Eucharistic ministers and distribute Holy Communion. Also, altar girls serve with altar boys in some Catholic churches.

But aside from some segments of the rabbinate and the Roman Catholic priesthood, it's not easy to think of job categories from which women are automatically barred. Embarking on a dream career is no longer the insurmountable barrier it once was for many women. It can, however, be impossible for a woman to get to the top—or even close to the top—in that career.

Getting Ahead

Women seeking careers in the business world know which companies are best to work for, which ones will offer them a real chance to make it all the way to the senior executive level. Such a company is Reebok, makers of shoes and other athletic equipment. Of Reebok's sixteen top executives in 1997, 44 percent were female. That gave Reebok the highest percentage of women executives of any U.S. corporation.

Another U.S. company with a good record of employing and promoting women is Avon, the door-to-door cosmetics sales firm. That's hardly surprising. Avon products are sold almost exclusively *by* women (3.2 million saleswomen worldwide) *to* women (who spent $4.8 billion on those products in 1996). You'd expect the company to have more than a token number of women in its executive suite, and it does. Of Avon's top executives, 29 percent were female in mid-1997. Three of those women were in line to be promoted to chief executive of the company when the president was scheduled to retire in 1998.

None of the three won the coveted promotion. Instead, Avon brought in an outsider, the former head of the Duracell battery company, to take over the top job. That outsider was a man.

"In the corporate world, women are great as 'seconds,'" fumed Judith Vladeck, a lawyer, when she heard the news. "Women are great as long as they make the men look good. Then when it comes to the top spots, they become invisible. Women are still in the support functions and men are seen as the leaders."[16]

Vladeck's words are echoed by other women struggling to climb the corporate ladder. When Pam was at the consulting firm, her privacy and self-respect certainly came in second to her boss's determination to get his hands on one of her files the instant he wanted to. Pam also cited the experience of her only female coworker, an older woman named Ronnie.

Ronnie had done well in the company. She had attained a job ranking equal to that of any of the men with whom she worked. She had her own clients, her own distinct areas of responsibility. But when it came time to redecorate the firm's offices, who was asked to set her own projects aside in order to pick out the new color scheme and furniture? Ronnie. Other women in business report being expected to "wait on" men in the office the way their wives or mothers might. Common requests include being asked to run errands for their male colleagues, or to prepare the coffee before a meeting. It doesn't matter what your job is or how many promotions you receive, these women say, if you continue to be treated as a second-class member of the working team.

Of course what happened to the women at Avon went beyond being treated as "seconds." Those women had been with the company for years. They were familiar with it and its products. They thoroughly understood how to direct a multimillion-member door-to-door sales force. Yet in the end, their expertise counted for nothing. They had made it almost all the way to the top. Then, at the last moment, they hit the glass ceiling. They were passed over in favor of someone whose previous work experience had centered not on cosmetics but on electric batteries. Someone whose sales know-how involved marketing through huge retail chain stores, rather than by means of Avon's direct-selling techniques. Someone who—probably not coincidentally—happened to be a man.

Judith Vladeck wasn't the only one expressing indignation at Avon's decision. Susan Bianchi-Sand, head of a Washington, D.C., group working to win equal pay for women, called the company's choice of a male chief executive shocking. "Here we have a business that makes its living off women," she exclaimed. If a woman executive is going to run into a glass ceiling at a female-friendly company like Avon, where can she possibly expect to succeed? People like Bianchi-Sand and Vladeck found the Avon case particularly devastating because it came at a time when more and more women did seem to be finding it easier to move up in the business world. "It's not a glass ceiling anymore," Vladeck concluded gloomily. "It's a cement ceiling."

But other women see matters differently. Sheila Wellington is the president of Catalyst, a New York group that researches women's issues. Wellington reminds people that Avon has been an "outstanding" workplace for women. Criticizing the company too strongly smacks of "picking on the good guys," she suggests. "Any way that you look at [Avon's] achievements for women," Wellington says, "they are absolutely stellar."

She has a point. Catalyst research shows that while there are 830 top executives in the nation's Fortune 500 companies, the number of females among them can be counted on one hand. The 500 largest U.S. corporations, as ranked by *Fortune* magazine, employed 825 male chairmen, chief executives, vice chairmen, presidents, and chief operating officers in 1997. They employed just five women of similar rank. That number hardly qualifies even as tokenism. Avon, Reebok, and a dozen other companies really are unusual in their willingness to hire and promote women.[17]

What's true in the business world tends to be true throughout the workplace. In research conducted for the National Science Foundation, Betty Vetter found that women scientists are not only underemployed compared with men, but also they are promoted less often and more slowly than their male colleagues. Women make up about 30 percent of all U.S. scientists, Vetter reports, but most are firmly lodged at or near the bottom of the employment ladder. Only a small number have reached the level of department head, laboratory director, or the like. Women "have been unable to pierce the upper scientific strata in anything beyond token numbers," she writes.[18]

It's the same story in the science departments of American colleges and universities, says Vetter. Women who teach science at the college level are twice as likely as men to be appointed to temporary, rather than permanent (tenured), positions. In chemistry, for example, women make up only 11 percent of tenured professors. The top ten U.S. college mathematics departments employed 303 tenured male professors in 1991 and only 4 females.[19] Although the number of women reaching high positions in the sciences and the academic world has grown in the 1990s, it still lags far behind the number of men. Overall, U.S. colleges and universities employed more than half a million male teachers in 1996 but only 387,000 female teachers.[20]

So far in this chapter, we have looked mostly at women whose jobs are professional or corporate. But what about the vast majority of American working women, the ones waiting on tables, assembling parts in a factory, or caring for the elderly in a nursing home? Does the glass ceiling affect them, too?

It does. Although most of the women who complain of the glass ceiling are in business and the professions, the same kind of artificial barriers that limit their career opportunities help perpetuate the pink-collar ghettos in which the majority of women spend their working lives.

How could they not? If the prejudice against women in the workplace is so strong that hardly any women make it to the top in the nation's largest corporations, isn't a similar prejudice apt to keep most women on the assembly line from reaching the level of factory manager? If a female scientist with a better academic record than many of her male colleagues cannot attain a tenured position, what are a female checkout clerk's chances of being promoted ahead of the men she works with? If competent professional women cannot win the respect of their male bosses, why should women who are expert taxi drivers or construction workers fare any better? Women in construction and on the assembly line may not do as much talking about the glass ceiling as business and professional women do. But they feel its effects—especially when it comes time for them to cash their paychecks.

The Pay Problem

If there is one issue that unites working women—from nurse's aide to high-powered executive to family doctor to office cleaner—it is the issue of pay. In 1997 the American Federation of Labor (AFL) and the Congress of Industrial Organizations (CIO), the nation's largest organized union of workers, surveyed their female membership. According to AFL-CIO findings, 94 percent of the country's five million unionized working women said that their top concern was ensuring that their pay was equal to that of male coworkers doing the same or similar jobs.[21]

That may seem odd. As we saw in the first chapter one prominent U.S. women's group claims that men and women do receive almost exactly equal wages. If that is true, it would be welcome news. In the past, as documented by historians Bonnie Anderson and Judith Zinsser, women have consistently earned from one-third to one-half less than boys and men. But according to the Independent Women's Forum, things have changed. Thanks to better educational opportunities and the determination to get ahead, Forum leaders say, today's young women have nearly overcome the wage gap. In 1997 U.S. women were earning 98¢ for every $1 earned by men.

Writing in *The Nation* magazine, columnist Katha Pollitt examined the research behind the Forum claim. That research consisted, she discovered, of a survey of working men and women age twenty-seven to thirty-three. None of those workers had ever had children. "What's wrong with this?" Pollitt asked.

The first thing that's wrong is that most women—76 percent— *have* had children by the age of thirty-three. So, probably, have most men. In excluding working parents from its survey, the Independent Women's Forum was ignoring three-quarters or more of all working men and women age twenty-seven to thirty-three.

And what about working men and women who hadn't yet celebrated their twenty-seventh birthdays? They were not included in the survey, either. Nor were workers between the ages of thirty-four and retirement. Any survey that looks at such a small percentage of the total group that it pretends to be studying is meaningless. So much for claims that, overall, working women are closing the wage gap.[22]

Why would the Independent Women's Forum publish such a flawed study? As a group, the Forum opposes new laws or other measures that would close the gap between men's and women's wages. Therefore, its survey was aimed at "proving" that no gap exists.

In fact, other figures suggest that the gap not only exists, but may actually be widening. According to the U.S. Department of Labor's Bureau of Labor Statistics, full-time working women in 1993 were earning 77¢ for every $1 earned by men. By 1997 women's pay had slipped to just under 75¢ for every $1 men were taking home.[23]

Why the disparity? To begin with, women in general do not reach the highest levels in the corporate and professional world. Naturally, their salaries are lower than those of the men who do make it to the top.

In addition, even when men and women do have the same job title and description, studies have shown that the women are likely to receive less pay than the men. Researchers at The Center for Creative Leadership of Greensboro, North Carolina, point out that in the late 1980s "women [were] still paid considerably less than men at their level."[24] In the early 1990s, Betty Vetter reported that while industrial chemists of both sexes started off at roughly the same salaries, they didn't end up with equal pay. By their mid-fifties, the men were earning nearly $80,000 a year. Women were getting just above $60,000. Vetter uncovered some other discouraging statistics. Women who worked as university assistant professors earned $1,873 less than their male counterparts, she found. Female associate professors earned $2,926 less. Women who attained the rank of full professor earned $6,500 less.[25] The more a female professor was promoted, in other words, the less she earned compared to males of equal rank!

A female doctor in one small New England city claims that little has changed since Vetter made her study. "We're not allowed to talk about our salaries," she says of the doctors in the medical group to which she belongs. This doctor is in her forties and has been with the group for several years. She is convinced that the keep-silent order comes because managers don't want it known that they try to attract young male doctors with salaries as high as, or higher than, those of the older women. "Why else would they be so secret?" she wonders. Pam says that at her consulting firm, many new employees were hired right out of college. Male graduates, she claims, were hired as associates; females as assistants. In business, as in the college or university, associate is a higher rank—with higher pay—than assistant.

Professional women are not the only ones who insist that they are being shortchanged on the job. More than a third of the women questioned in the 1997 AFL-CIO survey—many of whom work in shops and factories or as hotel maids and farm laborers—contended that they were not getting equal pay for equal work.[26] Even female athletes rarely earn as much as men. A star on one of the teams in the new Women's National Basketball Association can expect to be paid $50,000 or so a season. Male basketball stars figure their salaries in the millions. Of course, ticket sales are higher in the men's league. Only in such popular sports as ice skating, tennis, and gymnastics can women hope to equal men's earnings.

Other factors contribute to the pay disparity. Women are less likely than men to be paid for overtime work. They may also be excluded from some of the job "perks" that men enjoy. Businesswomen may not be invited along on high-status "conference weekends" at upscale golf clubs or beach resorts, for example. They may have smaller department or expense-account budgets than male co-workers. In 1996 Lorrie Beno was a saleswoman for Magna International, Inc., a large auto parts manufacturer based in Canada. That year, Beno pointed out to her bosses that while Magna salesmen had expense accounts of $40,000 or more a year, her allotment was just $6,000. How could she hope for high sales when she couldn't afford to entertain her clients in style? she demanded. Beno was quickly fired. She retaliated by suing Magna in court.[27]

Another perk that may not be extended to women is the year-end bonus.[28] Bonuses are especially important in the nation's leading financial corporations. Each of the few top managers at one such company can expect to take home as much as $25 million in bonus money come January. About two hundred partners—the level just below the top—can look forward to $4 million apiece. The company's 10,300 other employees may have to settle for bonuses ranging down to the $150,000 level.[29] Given the gender-based hiring and promotion patterns we've seen throughout this chapter, it's easy to figure which sex ends up with most of the cash.

But the overriding reason for the disparity between men's and women's wages is simply that so many women find themselves in low-paying jobs. Remember the statistics. Three-quarters of all U.S. working women are firmly entrenched in a pink-collar ghetto. They're baby-sitters, hairdressers, secretaries, housekeepers, supermarket checkout clerks. In the health-care field, women are overwhelmingly more likely to be nurses and lab assistants than doctors. Who are paid more, doctors or their helpers?

Not only do pink-collar ghetto jobs generally pay less than other kinds of jobs, but they may carry fewer benefits, such as pensions and health or life insurance. Pension and insurance plans are an essential part of a working person's total salary "package." Furthermore, jobs in the pink-collar ghetto are less likely than other types of employment to offer full-time work. A salesclerk may be hired on a temporary basis—during the tourist season or the winter holidays, for example—then let go when business drops off. Many part-time and temporary jobs pay only the minimum wage—$5.15 an hour in 1997. In the United States women fill a disproportionate number of such jobs.[30]

Fewer benefits compared with men, lower pay, slower promotions—that's the bad news for working women. More and better jobs in nearly every employment field is the good news. What's the rest of the story?

6

CONFLICTS AND PRESSURES

Brenda Barnes, corporate executive and mother of three, announced her decision in late September 1997. After twenty-two years of working at the Pepsi-Cola Company—the previous eighteen months as president and chief executive of Pepsi's entire North American division—Barnes had made up her mind to quit her job. For the time being, at least, she would stay at home full-time with her children, ages seven, eight, and ten.

Arriving at that decision had been a "traumatic" experience, Barnes admitted. "I have struggled with this for a long time." No wonder. Like others climbing the corporate ladder, Barnes had worked hard and made personal sacrifices on her way up. She had put in years of hectic traveling, dinner meetings, and late-night conferences. Sometimes she had to be out of town on her children's birthdays. At one point, she and her husband—who himself had resigned from PepsiCo three months earlier—had lived in separate cities in order to accommodate the demands of their jobs. Now, Brenda Barnes had had enough. "Every time you . . . miss a child's birthday, or a school concert or a parent-teacher discussion, you . . . feel the tug," she said. "I need to give my family more of my time."[1,2]

Not all working mothers would agree that Barnes had done the right thing. Some, as we will see, called her decision a blow to other women. But most could understand the "tug" she described. Balancing a job and a family can be a woman's toughest challenge.

Family Ties

It's a challenge few men ever have to face. Most men take it for granted that they will combine work with family life. Everyone else takes it for granted, too. In fact, many employers prefer to hire men with families than those without. A man who has a wife and children is usually regarded as more stable and more dependable than a bachelor. A woman, by contrast, may be perceived as less likely to be a reliable worker if she is married or has children. Even the prospect of hiring a young, single, childless woman for a professional or executive position may give an employer pause. She, too, is apt to wind up married, with a family. That could affect her job performance—or so many employers believe.

Why? Mixing work with motherhood can easily plunge a woman into the kind of conflict that eventually led to Brenda Barnes's resignation. As we have seen, most women, in most times and places, have functioned both as parents and as wage earners. So have most men. But while Western European and American societies have traditionally expected men to fill this dual role, they see it as less natural when women do the same. Women are meant to be mothers, first and foremost—that is the general idea. Anything that distracts a woman from her maternal duties may be regarded with suspicion. That is because society somehow assumes that mothers, not fathers, are the ones who bear the ultimate responsibility for their children's well-being. A 1997 tragedy illustrates how this assumption can play out in real life.

The stage was set for the tragedy when a Massachusetts couple hired a teenage girl to look after their two sons. Both the parents were doctors. The father had a full-time practice, but the mother had cut her work schedule down to three days a week. She even made time to come home most of those days to have lunch with her children and their sitter. Nevertheless, the sitter spent long hours alone with the two little boys. One day, apparently frustrated by the younger one's fussiness, she shook him violently. He died. The baby-sitter was charged with intentionally murdering the child, put on trial, and found guilty. (A judge later reduced the jury's verdict to involuntary manslaughter.)

The trial sparked wide interest and—despite the verdict—much public sympathy for the baby-sitter. It also unleashed a wave of anger directed against the dead child's mother. On radio call-in talk shows, in newspaper letters to the editor, and over the Internet, the popular verdict came in loud and clear. Morally, if not legally, the mother was as guilty as the baby-sitter.[3]

Why? Because she was at work when her baby died. Worse, she was at work by choice. Here was a woman who lived in a nice house in a nice suburb. She was married to a doctor. Obviously this mother wasn't working because her family needed the money. She was working because she wanted a career. She was working for her own personal satisfaction, selfishly ignoring her sons' needs. "She chose greed and not her children," in the words of one Internet user.[4]

But what about her husband? others demanded. He was also at work when his son was being shaken to death. He, like his wife, was building a career. He worked full-time, not part-time, although he, too, could probably have afforded to cut back on his hours. Yet no one ever suggested that he was in any way responsible for what happened. It was his wife's fault.

That's a stunning accusation. Still, it reflects society's thinking—and the deep-down feelings of many working mothers themselves. In the end, mothers are the ones held accountable for their children's welfare. If a woman works and her child suffers, she is likely to blame herself, at least in part. The magnitude of the problem this presents for women is made clear by a look at the statistics. Almost 60 percent of mothers return to work, full- or part-time, before their baby's first birthday.[5]

Of course, the number of women who "pay" for working by losing a child is extremely small. But every on-the-job mother knows what it is like to feel guilt over missing a parent-teacher conference, or sending a child to school with a cold because she can't take time off to stay home with him, or going to McDonald's for a birthday meal because she is too tired to throw a party. She knows about the flip side of the work-home conflict, as well: giving the party even though she's exhausted, losing a promotion because she had to take a week off when the kids had the flu, being docked a day's wages because she decided to skip work to take in a soccer game. At some point, every working mother feels, as Brenda Barnes did, torn between the demands of her family and those of her job.

But not every mother can afford to give up her job. In 1996 about eight million U.S. families were headed by single mothers.[6] Until that year, many single mothers received state and federal aid—welfare—to help them support their children. But the federal Welfare Reform Act of 1996 set strict limits on most such cash payments. Welfare recipients are now expected to find jobs. For America's eight million single mothers, a job is not a choice but a necessity.

It is a necessity, as well, for millions of married mothers whose husbands do not earn enough to support an entire family by themselves. Take Marlene Garrett, of Fort Lauderdale, Florida. Garrett has three children under the age of four. Her husband Rod brings home $250 a week from his job making hospital curtains. The Garretts pay $400 a month in rent. They owe $5,000 in back medical bills. They have no health insurance and no car. Marlene Garrett's $6-an-hour job at a bagel cafe is the key to survival for this family.[7]

Other mothers believe they have equally good reasons for working. One is saving money for her children's education. Another keeps her job because it carries better health and pension benefits than her husband's. A third works to finance family vacations or pay the mortgage. Those are all good reasons for going out to work. Or maybe a woman feels more secure when she's working. What if her husband dies, she may ask herself, or there is a divorce? She had better be prepared with up-to-date job skills and a solid résumé. Some women work because they want to use their talents to carve out a successful business or professional career. Why not? Men do it all the time. Then again, consider an athlete. Sheryl Swoopes was the mother of a month-old baby when she began trying for a permanent playing spot on the Houston Comets of the Women's National Basketball Association.[8] A person who hopes to make it in the sports world can hardly put her career on hold while she devotes herself full-time to motherhood. No one would dream of asking a male athlete to take a career break when he becomes a father.

Still, no matter how often a mother tells herself that she has very good reasons for working, she must remain aware of society's views—and her own—on maternal responsibility. "If my finances permitted, I'd love to stay home," Marlene Garrett says. "Who's a better caretaker than Mom?"

The Child-Care Crisis

Certainly not Vivienne, the caretaker Garrett employs. Vivienne's apartment is clean and neat. But there are no toys or books in it. The Garrett children spend ten hours a day in front of Vivienne's television set. "It breaks my heart, leaving them there," Garrett told a news reporter. "I want them in a learning environment. This is the best I can do right now. It's an emergency situation."

A "perpetual emergency" is how experts describe the day-care situation for low-income working mothers.[9] Generally, such a mother's best hope is to enroll her children in a state-licensed day-care center.

To be licensed, a center must meet certain standards of cleanliness, provide a specified ratio of care-givers to children enrolled, and so forth. However, licensing standards vary. One state may require one adult to be present for every three infants. Another may allow one person to care for as many as eight. A state may mandate that day-care providers receive "training," without being clear as to what that training should entail. "In most states," reports *The New York Times*, "it is easier to become a child-care worker than to obtain a driver's license."[10]

Another day-care problem is its cost. Marlene Garrett cannot afford the $270 a week she would have to pay to put her three youngsters in a licensed center. The 1996 Welfare Reform Act required states to spend more on day care, but most state money goes to help former welfare recipients pay for child care. Women like Garrett, who have never been on welfare, get no help.[11] Some make do with a baby-sitter like Vivienne. Others turn to a patchwork of friends and relatives: Grandma takes the kids on Monday and Wednesday, Aunt Sue looks after them on Tuesday and Friday, and neighbors help out on Thursday. Older brothers and sisters may be pressed into baby-sitting service as well. Some mothers rely on unlicensed day-care providers—and trust that their children will be well cared-for.

All too often, that trust is misplaced. It's estimated that 60 percent of U.S. children under age six are in some form of day care. Researchers at Yale University in New Haven, Connecticut, found that the quality of care at 86 percent of the day-care centers they studied ranged from poor to mediocre.[12] One Florida day-care center—shut down by the state in 1995—consisted of a single woman with twenty children under the age of four in her trailer home. Two of the children had chicken pox. All were hungry. Their only entertainment was TV.[13]

Of course, not all working mothers put their children in day-care centers, licensed or not. Some leave them at home alone, with a neighbor to "check in" occasionally, while they try to earn a few dollars. Many American children are "latchkey kids," returning home from school each day before their parents come home from work. Other mothers can afford a private, at-home, baby-sitter. That's not always an ideal solution, either, as we saw earlier in this chapter. A growing number of parents are relying on hidden cameras to "keep an eye" on the sitters they hire.

Add the dilemmas of child care—where to find it, how to afford it, wondering whether it's safe—to the tug most women feel as they wave goodbye to their children, and it becomes easy to see why any working mother may sometimes appear to her boss as being distracted on the job. And bear in mind that children are only one aspect of family life. Women have other responsibilities as well.

Other Family Obligations

At some point, most women will find themselves having to care for an elderly parent or other relative. Just as society assumes that mothers are more responsible than fathers for their children, so it expects daughters, rather than sons, to provide elder care as needed. Elder care can involve shopping, cooking, and cleaning for someone who finds it hard to get around. It can mean accompanying someone on trips to the doctor. Often, a woman finds it necessary to care for an elderly parent in her own home. That can be an extraordinarily stressful and time-consuming task.

Even marriage is different for working men and women. Most wives contribute to helping their husbands get ahead on the job. Maybe the contribution consists of having the boss over to dinner. Perhaps it involves running the accounting side of a husband's business, or agreeing to move to another part of the country where he's been offered a better job. How many men agree to relocate so their wives can win a promotion? Susan Borman, wife of the former U.S. astronaut and Eastern Airlines executive Frank Borman, contends that no corporate executive can hope to succeed without a family's help. "Families pay the price," she says. Male executives "have had mothers, fathers, wives and children supporting them all the way."

Others concede the point. In a 1997 divorce case, a Connecticut judge awarded one ex-wife half of her former husband's money and other assets. He also gave her a share of his future pension— $20 million in all. The judge seemed to agree with the wife that she had contributed as much as her husband had to his success. She had helped pay his way through business school. She had given up her teaching job to raise the couple's two daughters. She had created and maintained a lovely home, entertained her husband's business associates, and lent him her support by going along on business trips.[14] That's the level of support a corporate executive needs. How many working wives get it from their husbands?

How many husbands of working women contribute equally to doing household chores? According to one study, U.S. women who don't have outside jobs spend eight hours a day on housework. Full-time working women put in five hours a day.[15] In many households, the missing three hours of work probably gets done skimpily, if at all. "Most men . . . seem to think food magically appears in a refrigerator," one woman executive told researchers for The Center for Creative Leadership. "They can't comprehend chores." Another pointed out that after spending the week in the office, she makes a point of devoting weekends to housework and children. "My husband doesn't do this," she went on. "He will be out of town all week and then play golf on Saturday."

The fact that women with full-time jobs may also do most of the housework, be expected to sacrifice for the sake of a spouse's career, and assume responsibility for ensuring safe child and elder care are just some of the obstacles they face as they strive to succeed in the workplace. Others stem from the fact that employers are fully aware of how tough those obstacles are for women to deal with. That awareness itself plays a part in keeping the glass ceiling firmly in place.

"There was a task force put together that I heard about just by accident," a female executive recalls. "I was the logical person to run it, so I didn't understand why I hadn't been told about it." The woman questioned her bosses. They explained that the position would involve extensive travel. "Because I was married, they assumed I wouldn't be willing to be away from home (or my husband wouldn't let me)." That woman had bumped into a glass ceiling constructed from her male bosses' conviction that a wife belongs at home with her husband. Imagine those same bosses denying a man a promotion because it would take him away from his wife!

Diane M. Silberstein, a former vice president at *The New Yorker* magazine, claims that another set of assumptions led to her collision with the glass ceiling. She was dismissed from her job, she says, after she told her boss that she was expecting her second child. According to Silberstein, her boss said he thought she was not planning to have any more children. He displayed "obvious disapproval," she says. He warned her that she was "underestimating the difficulty of balancing the responsibilities of a second child and a publisher's position." Silberstein took *The New Yorker* to court in an effort to get her job back. (*The New Yorker* emphatically denies that Silberstein was fired because of her pregnancy.)[16]

Whatever the truth behind what happened at *The New Yorker*, it is a fact that even the remote possibility of a pregnancy can scare off a prospective employer. Janet M. Clarke discovered that in 1997. A forty-four-year-old banking executive, Clarke was being considered for a position as a director in a large U.S. chemical company. "Do you plan to have children?" one of her interviewers—a seventy-two-year-old man—wanted to know. Outraged by the question, Clarke snapped back that she was about to become a stepgrandmother. "Should I bring him or her to a board meeting?" she demanded acidly. Clarke failed to win the directorship.[17]

Traditional ideas about women and the work-home conflicts

they face are not the only factors that help maintain the glass ceiling. Other prejudices continue to hurt women in the workplace.

Facing Prejudice

It's not easy for women to break into—and succeed in—a male-dominated field. Jane Perlov, now a chief of detectives in New York City, discovered that when she joined the police department in 1981. Once, as a rookie, Perlov was the only woman participating in a nighttime drug raid in a dangerous neighborhood. Entering the suspected drug den, Perlov and the male officers with her found their way blocked by a locked metal door. For the men, it was testing time. "Jane, why don't you kick it in?" one of them asked. Perlov knew she had to pass the test—or forget about trying to make it on the force. "So I closed my eyes and thought of every John Wayne movie I'd ever seen," she says today. "And I kicked it. And it opened."[18] Perlov was on her way.

Women like Perlov who embark on careers that call for physical strength are commonly regarded by their male colleagues as incapable of doing the work, at least at first. It is true that women, on average, are smaller and less muscular than men. Still, most do manage to kick the door open—or do whatever else it takes for them to prove themselves on the job. In some instances, being smaller can be an advantage. A female firefighter may be able to squeeze through a narrow window or doorway where a man might not, for example.

What is more, when it comes to physical endurance, many women perform as well as—or better than—men. Just look at female athletes.

A century ago, it was considered unladylike for a woman to do anything much more athletic than take a walk. As late as 1942, U.S. sports officials refused to sanction a women's 100-yard dash. Too demanding a race for the "weaker sex."[19] Twenty-five years later, women were competing in the 100-yard dash—but still being told that they were not "physiologically able" to take part in long-distance events such as marathons. When one defiant woman did show up at the 1967 Boston Marathon, race officials tried to throw her out. Finally, in 1984 the first women's Olympic marathon was introduced. The winner's time of 2 hours, 24 minutes, 52 seconds still stands as the women's Olympic record. It was a time that would have beaten thirteen of twenty previous men's Olympic marathon winners. Dogsled racer Susan Butcher has won Alaska's grueling 1,150-mile (2,414-kilometer) Iditarod four times. The Iditarod, like a growing number of endurance events, is open to both sexes.[20]

Yet the perception that women are not physically as tough as men persists. In her study for the National Science Foundation, Betty Vetter found that women applying for jobs as engineers are often turned down by prospective employers who contend that engineering demands more physical strength than women possess. Women may also be told that they are unfit for an engineering job because it requires so much outdoor work.[21] Women prefer to work inside. Anyway, that's the assumption.

Along with being told that they are not physically tough enough for a particular job, women may be told that they are not mentally tough enough. "Women are traditionally perceived as weak," say researchers at The Center for Creative Leadership. Many men see women executives as having less of a commitment to the job than they have themselves. Many assume that compared with men, women are less able to deal with stress, less self-confident, less intellectual, less rational—the list goes on and on. By the same token, many assume that women are more "people-oriented" than men. Women, they believe, are more caring, patient, tolerant, and understanding than men.

In fact, neither set of assumptions is true, Center researchers have concluded. According to the personality measurements they made, male and female executives score almost identically when it comes to self-control, security, rationality, and all the rest. Their scores are equally close with regard to patience and understanding. Similar findings come from Catalyst, the New York women's research group. "Gender differences in managerial style may be mainly in the eye of the beholder," Catalyst says.[22] As far as commitment to a job is concerned, it is worth remembering that Brenda Barnes's husband quit his PepsiCo job three months *before* she quit hers. And don't forget that the "test" Jane Perlov was put to in that drug den was a test of mental, as well as physical, toughness. It was a test she passed easily.

Interestingly, the very words often used to describe working men and women indicate how deeply ingrained some negative attitudes toward women really are. "Men are called leaders," says one senior female executive. "Women are called bossy. I have always felt that if a woman wants something done then she is nagging, if a man wants something done, then he is being constructive and showing initiative."[23]

Other women have noticed the same language shifts. "Why am I called an egotist?" demands singer, actress, and director Barbra Streisand. She knows that the word is meant as a put-down. The dictionary defines *egotist* as a conceited, boastful person. "Is it because I dare to do more than one job? Why isn't Kevin Costner called an egotist for acting and directing his own movies? Or Mel Gibson?" Streisand answers her own question. "It's a sexist attitude, that's all."[24]

Sexist is a word that pops up frequently in discussions about the glass ceiling. Like a racist, a sexist is a person with irrational prejudices—in this case, against members of the opposite sex. Of all the sexist attitudes that confront women in the workplace, perhaps the one they find most infuriating is the idea that they are "too emotional."

Sometimes, "too emotional" translates into "apt to burst into tears." Astronaut Sally Ride was at a news conference with several of her male colleagues when a reporter asked if she ever cried during training. Grinning at the men around her, Ride demanded to know why that question wasn't being directed at them.[25] Her good-humored response left the reporter looking silly.

At other times, "too emotional" means "short-tempered" or "likely to fly off the handle." One women says wryly, "My boss can yell and pound his fist on the table. I can't yell—it wouldn't be accepted."[26] Of course it would be equally unacceptable for her to cry. Actually, according to both Catalyst and The Center for Creative Leadership, she is no more likely than a man to feel the need to do either one.

The fact that working women are not as overly emotional as they are reputed to be is in itself surprising. That's because many women work under greater pressure than their male colleagues.

Pressure, Pressure, Pressure

"All of the female executives we interviewed differed from their male counterparts in one fundamental way," reports The Center for Creative Leadership. "Throughout their careers, they had to operate with three levels of pressure constantly pushing on them."

The first level consists of the pressure of the job itself, which both male and female executives share. The second level—the pressure of the work-home conflict—is felt mainly by women. The third level of pressure is experienced almost exclusively by women who have chosen to work in a "man's field." It comes from the sense of being a pioneer in the workplace.

"Women are a minority is this business," explains one of the female executives in the Center's study. "A woman coming into a high-level meeting will see few other women. . . . They feel distinctly different."

Besides feeling out of place as the first—or only—woman in a particular workplace, such a woman may see herself as having an obligation to future generations of women. "I feel that if I fail, it will be a long time before they hire another woman for the job," a woman told Creative Leadership interviewers.[27] "There is this pressure to prove yourself as you're a woman and breaking ground for future women," a female engineer informed another group of researchers.[28]

It is because so many working women regard themselves and others like them as role models for younger women that Brenda Barnes's resignation from PepsiCo provoked criticism. Here was a smart, savvy woman who had already outperformed most of the men around her. Everyone expected her to rise even higher in the company.

And then she quit. "This has set the rest of us back a long time," mourned a New York marketing consultant. "It verifies all the worst stereotypes about women in the workplace." As she saw it, Barnes's resignation would make it that much easier for employers to go on denying jobs and promotions to working mothers— or to women who might become mothers. Perhaps her quitting would even inspire other working mothers to hand in their own resignations.[29] Brenda Barnes had failed as a role model.

Ironically, Barnes's experience mirrors that of the Massachusetts mother whose baby died at the hands of his baby-sitter. Like that mother, Barnes was only doing what her husband had also done. Both the Barneses resigned from Pepsi. Both the Massachusetts doctors worked. But no one blamed the dead child's father for working, and no one called Randall Barnes a poor role model. In each case, the criticism landed elsewhere.

To the three levels of pressure on working women listed by The Center for Creative Leadership, it is possible to add a fourth. That is the pressure women feel from male colleagues who are made uneasy by their presence or who feel insecure because of it.

Remember Pam, who left her job at a New York City consulting firm because of the company's "boys' club" atmosphere? The sense of isolation and lack of respect she was made to feel was a form of that sort of pressure. It is a pressure familiar to many working women.

"I think socializing is one area where there are problems being a woman in a man's world," says one woman. "Men really do prefer other men, they feel very comfortable with other men." This woman knows they feel less comfortable with her, but she is not about to let them squeeze her out of the picture. "They would prefer to leave me out when it comes to a drink with the boys at lunchtime, but I insist on going because that is where all the work is done."[30]

This woman has the right attitude. A lot of business is conducted in restaurants and on golf courses, and women need to be part of the action. Not being included can hurt their chances of meeting the people and striking the deals they need to succeed on the job. Until a few years ago, women were not merely left out when it came to company socializing; they were flatly refused admission to many "men-only" eating places and country clubs. Women successfully sued the segregated facilities under antidiscrimination laws. Today, only a handful of private clubs in a few states remain off-limits to women.

Even informal get-togethers around the water cooler or in an employee lounge must be open to women if women are to be successful in the workplace. It is at such spots that employees "network," exchanging gossip and information about what's going on in a company. It is where they learn who is about to be promoted and who may be planning to leave. It is where they hear about upcoming opportunities for promotions or new job responsibilities.

Informal settings are also where younger workers have a chance to get to know older, more experienced company employees. Often, an older worker will become the friend and mentor— trusted advisor—of a younger one. A mentor can help an unsure junior employee figure out the most promising career path to follow, suggest work options to explore, and point out opportunities to get ahead. When women are cut off from company networking, and company mentors—as Pam was in her consulting job—their chances for job advancement fade.

Deeper Resentment

In some workplaces, sexism goes well beyond being excluded from mentoring and networking. When Brenda Berkman became one of the first women in the New York City Fire Department, some of the men she was supposed to be working with ignored her totally, refusing to eat with her or even to speak to her. But that was hardly the worst of it. "I got death threats at my home," she says now.[31]

Why so much animosity? Part of the answer probably has to do with the unease many people feel when they are forced to face change. In the early 1980s no woman had ever served as a New York firefighter. Berkman changed that, and some men resented her for it. The result: rude behavior—even criminal threats.

Very likely the threats came from men who themselves felt threatened. A profound reason for the animosity of some men toward female workplace pioneers is fear. When a woman enters what was formerly an all-male workplace, the men she encounters may see her as a danger to their very livelihoods.

Some men worry that women will steal their jobs outright. "There would be plenty of jobs for men if women would just stay at home," is a familiar theme.[32] Actually, the problem for men is a bit more subtle.

As we have noted throughout this book, women traditionally have been paid less than men for doing similar work. At the same time, fields in which women dominate—elementary education, nursing, social work—generally pay less than fields in which men dominate—college teaching, doctoring, construction. So when women appear in what has always been an exclusively male working environment, that could signal a drop in wages for everyone.

It has in the past. When eighteenth- and nineteenth-century factory owners in Europe and America began hiring female workers, they paid the women less than their male employees. The fact that women were forced, by law or necessity, to accept the lower wages enabled employers to keep the men's salaries where they were. If the men demanded raises, the boss could threaten to replace them with still more low-paid women. He could use the same threat to force male workers to accept wage reductions. As historians Bonnie Anderson and Judith Zinnser put it, "The entry of women usually meant a downgrading of work and wages [for both sexes]."[33]

A similar downgrading may be going on right now in one formerly all-male preserve—the clergy. The number of female Protestant ministers and Jewish rabbis soared in the 1990s. Some fear that if the trend continues, the field will become a new pink-collar ghetto. "Men are withdrawing [from religious vocations]," warns Judith Berling, dean of the Graduate Theological Union in Berkeley, California. "[Men are] looking for the prestige and money that leads to the good life. In their place, women . . . are moving in."[34]

Something similar could happen in the business world, particularly in its lower ranks. As one executive told The Center for Creative Leadership, "Women work harder and for less money. Women will accept pay cuts [for a chance to get ahead]. . . . This is an advantage because senior management wants the best for the least price." Another confessed to interviewers one reason she thought she, rather than a man, was hired for her job: "I was cheap."[35] Small wonder if some men feel insecure as more and more women show up in the workplace.

Sexual Harassment

Sometimes, a man's economic insecurity and the resentment he feels toward working women will lead him into the extreme form of behavior that has come to be called sexual harassment.

The term was coined in the 1970s. Today, the federal Equal Employment Opportunity Commission defines sexual harassment as "sexual advances, requests for sexual favors, and other verbal or physical conduct of a sexual nature." Although figures vary, studies suggest that between 20 and 35 percent of women in the U.S. civilian workforce have experienced what they consider to have been such harassment.[36,37] Among women in the armed forces, the percentage is higher. A 1997 government investigation showed that 47 percent of Army women complain of having been sexually harassed.[38] Under federal law, both military and civilian women are entitled to have their sexual harassment cases heard in a court of law.

To date, the U.S. legal system has recognized two distinct types of sexual harassment. In the first, women are the objects or victims of direct sexual abuse. Women at a Mitsubishi auto plant in Illinois, for example, claimed that their male coworkers had taped them to factory carts, demanded sex, and threatened to kill them. The women won their case.[39] In 1998 the EEOC brought suit against Astra U.S.A., a subsidiary of a Swedish firm. The suit was filed on behalf of eighty former Astra employees. Those employees were all women. All were either mothers or middle-aged. All had been fired and their jobs given to attractive younger women. The "jobs" of the new employees—for which the fired women had been deemed unsuitable—included partying with, and dating, male executives. Astra settled with the EEOC for a record $10 million.[40]

The second type of sexual harassment recognized by the courts is based on the idea of a "hostile workplace." Tammy Blakey, a pilot for Continental Airlines, cited such hostility in a 1997 lawsuit. According to Blakey, male pilots were displaying pornographic pictures prominently in airplane cockpits. Even when she objected, the men refused to take the pictures down. The sight of them caused her so much emotional distress that she was unable to do her job, Blakey claimed. She won a quarter of a million dollars in damages.[41]

But other types of harassment have gone unpunished. In a New Jersey case, a female electrician sued on the grounds that the men she worked with laughed and swore at her as she struggled to unload heavy boxes. She also complained that higher-ups refused to put a lock on the door of the shower she and another woman used. Harassment, but not sexual harassment, the judge said, dismissing her case.

A Rhode Island judge reacted similarly in a separate case: A woman claimed that the men she worked with had made disparaging remarks about working women and interfered with her efforts to do her job. They had sabotaged her projects before she could complete them. The judge had no doubt that the woman had suffered exactly the kind of treatment she described. But that treatment did not involve sex itself. Therefore it was not "sexual harassment as that term has come to be defined," he ruled.

Perhaps the definition needs changing. That suggestion comes from Vicki Schultz, a professor of law at Yale University. As Schultz sees it, the current definition puts too much emphasis on sex and not enough on harassment. A woman who is forced to listen to belittling remarks about her capabilities, intelligence, and human integrity is every bit as much a victim of sexual harassment as a woman who is faced with pornography or an amorous boss, Schultz believes.[42] By the same token, having her work undermined by jealous or insecure men is just as damaging to her as being denied a promotion because she is pregnant, or getting a smaller paycheck because of her sex. All are forms of gender-based discrimination. Women who suffer any of them should be able to find protection under the law.

Making sure they do find protection is Vicki Schultz's goal—and the goal of millions of other women. It is the goal of many men, as well.

So it should be. Only when working women are treated, paid, and promoted on an equal footing with men—only when the glass ceiling is truly shattered—will men be free of the fear that female coworkers can undercut their wages and threaten their livelihoods. When that fear is gone, everyone will be better off.

7

DISMANTLING
THE GLASS CEILING

"The glass ceiling has certainly been shattered," U.S. Air Force Secretary Sheila Widnall enthusiastically informed a group of women meeting in New York City in mid-1996.

"It's not a glass ceiling anymore," lawyer Judith Vladeck said glumly a few months later. "It's a cement ceiling." Vladeck had just learned that the Avon cosmetic company had passed over three of its own top-ranked women to hire a new *male* chief executive.

Vladeck was exaggerating. A cement ceiling? With more women than ever before filling the interesting, well-paid jobs that, a decade or so earlier, were reserved entirely for men? With working women winning perks and promotions in record numbers? With women participating more fully than ever at the highest levels of public life? Nonsense!

But Sheila Widnall was overstating her case, as well. Even though women have broken into nearly every job category there is, all too often they are present in mere token numbers. Very few women have a chance of reaching the pinnacle in any career field. Many see their careers falter as they struggle to resolve work-home conflicts. Millions are mired in low-prestige pink-collar ghettos. Overall, U.S. working women earn just three-quarters of what men earn. The glass ceiling shattered? No. Being dismantled, perhaps. Disappearing bit by bit. But not yet gone.

Who will eventually tear it down? Women themselves will lead the way, of course, but their employers can help. So can people in the media and in civic organizations. So can government.

Equal Opportunity and Affirmative Action

Let's start with government. It was the federal government that did so much to open doors to U.S. working women with the Civil Rights Act of 1964. That law banned sex discrimination in the workplace. It also created the Equal Employment Opportunity Commission.

We have already seen how the EEOC, initially prodded by activist groups like the National Organization for Women, has battled workplace discrimination. When working women feel they have been mistreated, they may ask the EEOC to look into their complaint. That is what happened when dozens of women were fired from Astra U.S.A. and replaced by younger women. EEOC staff members began their investigation in May 1996. They quickly found that male Astra executives had created "an organized pattern of sexual harassment." The EEOC's next step was to begin a lawsuit on behalf of the fired women. Before the case could go to trial, however, Astra officials agreed to the $10 million settlement.[1]

It's not uncommon for EEOC investigations to work out this way. Rather than spend millions of dollars defending itself in court, a company that knows that the EEOC has a strong case against it will settle before the suit can be heard. By the mid-1990s the EEOC was becoming increasingly active in the fight against discrimination. The number of lawsuits brought by the commission on behalf of employees more than doubled between 1993 and 1997.

One of those suits involved Home Depot, the discount building-supply chain. Women who worked at Home Depot stores in eight Western states claimed that the company favored men in its hiring and promotion policies. Whereas women were assigned to work cash registers, they said, male employees were sent onto the sales floor. Their job was to talk with customers, offer them building advice, and suggest which products they might buy. Those sales-floor jobs were the ones that led to promotions and pay raises, the women pointed out. Cash-register jobs led nowhere. Even women with construction experience were routinely denied the better positions, the complainants added.

The EEOC found that the women had a valid case, and Home Depot agreed to a $87.5 million settlement. More important, the company promised to change its discriminatory policies. From now on, women working at Home Depot stores in every part of the country should be getting more equal treatment. Other companies that have recently reached sex- or race-discrimination settlements with the EEOC include the Lucky Stores, Safeway, Texaco, and Publix Supermarkets.[2]

But while the EEOC is making new inroads against workplace discrimination, another government antidiscrimination tool appears to be in danger of falling into disuse. That tool is affirmative action.

Like so much else in the fight against discrimination, affirmative action originated in the 1960s. It was designed to work in tandem with the Civil Rights Act of 1964. But unlike that law, which forbade discrimination in the *present*, affirmative action policies were intended to undo the effects of discrimination in the *past*.

Affirmative action meant reaching out to women, blacks, and members of other racial or ethnic minorities, and drawing them into the mainstream of American life. Under affirmative-action policies, schools and businesses that received any amount of federal money were required to report the sexual and ethnic makeup of their student bodies and workforces. If a pattern of discrimination emerged, the school or business had to submit integration goals, along with a schedule for meeting those goals.[3] Following the federal government's lead, many states and cities established affirmative-action plans of their own.

For years, affirmative action seemed to be doing its job of promoting diversity. In the 1970s, for example, the San Francisco Fire Department refused even to accept job applications from women. Not until 1987 did the department take on its first female employees. In the 1990s, 16 percent of new firefighters being hired were women.[4]

But affirmative action was already coming under fire. By ensuring that women got 16 percent of new jobs, the San Francisco Fire Department was simultaneously ensuring that a certain percentage of male applicants would *not* get those jobs. It was a similar story when it came to reserving job spaces for minority-group members. Before long, the racial and sexual battle lines were being drawn. Whites who had been passed over for jobs went to court claiming that they had been treated unfairly because of their race. Hispanic Americans challenged blacks who—according to them—had been given preferential treatment. Men challenged women.

The outcomes of the various court cases produced mostly confusion. In some instances, judges backed affirmative-action policies; in others, they struck them down. Finally, one state, California, decided to act on its own. In 1996 voters there agreed to put an end to all public affirmative-action programs in the state. The ban went into effect the next year.[5]

The California vote did not end the confusion, however. Despite the new state ban on affirmative action, officials in large California cities like San Francisco and Los Angeles said they would continue trying to find ways to lend a helping hand to women and minorities hoping to enter the workforce. And in Houston, voters rejected a ballot proposal that would have ended that city's programs of affirmative action. Houston's endorsement of affirmative action came just weeks after California's rejection of it became legal.[6]

To complicate matters further, a nationwide poll taken late in 1997 showed that while most people in the United States dislike affirmative-action plans, they do support affirmative-action goals. In other words, Americans as a whole support an end to discrimination. But they don't want to see it ended through a series of rules that are themselves based on racial and sexual standards.[7] Needless to say, the future of affirmative action remains very much up in the air.

Title IX

Another federal antidiscrimination weapon that has produced mixed results goes by the name of Title IX, which prohibits gender discrimination at any educational institution that receives federal funds. Although Title IX addresses every aspect of education, it has come to be applied primarily to athletic programs in the nation's high schools, colleges, and universities.

Title IX seems simple enough. The law requires college athletic departments to provide comparable programs for male and female students. If the college supports ten or a dozen women's sports teams, it must support ten or a dozen men's teams. If it offers modern sports facilities and well-groomed fields for men, it must do likewise for women. If it spends a certain amount of money on sports for one sex, it must spend approximately the same amount on sports for the other sex.

Yet simple as the law sounds, U.S. college athletic departments seem to be having difficulty understanding it. A 1997 survey by the National Collegiate Athletic Association (NCAA) showed that two-thirds of U.S. college athletes were men. Only one-third were women. This in spite of the fact that women make up half of the nation's total college population. What is more, colleges were spending an average of $663,000 a year on women's sports. They were spending more than three times that amount—$2.4 million a year—on men's sports. "Pathetic," is how Christine Grant, director of women's athletics at the University of Iowa, describes college compliance with Title IX.

How do the colleges get away with it? Until now, administrators at the U.S. Office for Civil Rights, which is charged with enforcing Title IX, have been lax in monitoring compliance. They have been satisfied with assurances from college athletic directors that they intend to expand women's sports programs in the future. They have accepted the argument that even though a women's program is smaller and less well-funded than a men's program, women at a particular school have all the sports opportunities they need.[8]

The U.S. Office for Civil Rights promises to get tougher in the future. But even if it does, the NCAA estimates that it will take until the year 2007 to achieve gender equality in college sports.[9]

Other Government Involvement

What else can government—federal, state, and local—do to help dismantle the glass ceiling? In 1993 President Bill Clinton signed the Family Leave Act into law. That law allows workers to take time off to care for a child, parent, or spouse during a medical emergency. Workers receive no pay for the hours or days they are not at work. But neither may their employers fire them when they call in to say they can't show up.

The federal law applies only to companies with more than fifty employees. Some states have more generous laws. In Maine, for example, a worker in a company with as few as fifteen employees may take up to ten weeks of unpaid leave to deal with a family medical emergency. He or she is entitled to the same amount of time off for the birth or adoption of a child.[10]

In the area of child care, too, local, state, and federal governments can intervene to reduce the work-home conflict that so many working mothers feel. As we know, the Welfare Reform Act of 1996 required states to provide more child-care benefits to working mothers who are former welfare recipients. But that law did little to help low-income women who have never been on welfare. Early in 1998 President Clinton announced a plan to target this group. He called on Congress to raise federal child-care spending from $3 billion to $7.5 billion over the following five years. Doing so would double—from one million to two million—the number of children in government-subsidized day-care centers.

At the same time, President Clinton asked Congress to cut taxes for working parents who pay for their own day care. Altogether, Clinton's program of tax cuts and day-care subsidies would cost the nation $21 billion over five years.[11] Many in Congress objected to the proposal. Some thought it too expensive. Others argued against any expansion of the federal government's role in providing day care.

No matter how a person may feel about government involvement in day care, it is clearly up to federal authorities to resolve another problem associated with the glass ceiling. That problem is sexual harassment and misconduct in the armed forces. Being the victim of such activity has cost more than one military woman her career.

In 1997 a government commission appointed to look into the problem released its report. Its conclusion that harassment and misconduct are widespread in the U.S. military came as no surprise. The panel's suggestion for dealing with the problem, however, astonished many Americans. Panel members recommended that male and female recruits be kept apart, especially during basic training.

"A slap in the face to women." That's how Carolyn B. Maloney, a U.S. representative from New York, greeted the suggestion. Senator Olympia J. Snowe of Maine reacted in much the same way. "I think it sends the wrong message about the direction we need to take in the military," Snowe said. "Why create this separateness, this barrier almost from the outset?" Such a barrier can only hurt women in the military, she and others believe. Separation would "diminish the opportunities for women" in the military, cautioned another New York representative, Nita M. Lowey.

As if to confirm her words, a measure of support for the panel's recommendation came from the Center for Military Readiness. That group strongly opposes expanding the role of women in the armed forces. Its president, Elaine Donnelly, called the segregation recommendation "a modest step in the right direction."

One woman who knew exactly what Donnelly meant—and didn't like the implication—was Evelyn P. Foote. "It's going backwards," she declared. Foote is a retired brigadier general with a thirty-year army career behind her. Training men and women separately, she maintains, is apt to end with their having different types of skills and specialties. If that happens, the military could revert to something like the sex-segregated armed forces of previous decades. Men will be taking the risks, making the strategic decisions, and issuing the commands. Women will be answering phones and providing backup for the men. They will be taking orders, not giving them. As in the old days of the WACs and the WAVES, women will languish in the lower ranks. "I feel like I'm back in the early '60s," Foote said in disgust.[12]

Women-Friendly Employers

Like government, employers who want to help women battle the glass ceiling have a choice of directions in which to move. They can adopt policies that encourage the hiring and promoting of more women. Or they can make it easier for women to do their jobs by providing such amenities as emergency leave or company-funded day-care centers. Ideally, of course, they can do both.

Avon is one company often singled out for its support of women who are eager to rise in the corporate ranks. Even after Avon failed to promote a woman to the job of chief executive,

Sheila Wellington of the Catalyst research group referred to the company as "stellar" for women. With 29 percent of its top management female, Avon stands in eleventh place among large U.S. companies with the greatest share of women in corporate offices.

Companies boasting even higher percentages include Reebok International; Pitney Bowes, which produces office equipment; the Student Loan Marketing Association; and Corestates, a financial company. In each of these companies, 40 percent or more of top management is female.[13] Smaller businesses may also have hiring and promotion policies that help women who want to get ahead. At Little Caesars Pizza stores, 50 percent of managers are women. Centura Health, a Denver health-care network, has filled three of its fifteen vice-presidential slots with women. In all, 64 percent of Centura management is female.

Along with more promotions go higher pay and increased benefits, like health insurance and pension plans. One company frequently cited for its benefits is 3M. With headquarters in Maplewood, Minnesota, 3M produces drugstore products and reflective traffic materials as well as its more familiar office and computer supplies.

Benefits at 3M don't stop at health and pension plans. Others are aimed specifically at attracting—and keeping—female employees. They include a healthy-baby program of pregnancy and newborn care; sick-child-care coverage; a referral program for mothers looking for day care; and a company-sponsored kindergarten. In addition, the company provides online advice for employees seeking elder care, and offers financial aid and counseling to those coping with a death in the family.

3M is not the only corporation that extends such benefits to working women. The Nike footwear company has on-site day care, a baby-sitting center for school-age children, and a kids' sports program. It assists couples seeking to adopt a child. (Nike, however, has been criticized for its poor treatment of women workers in its Asian factories.)[14] Little Caesars Pizza also offers adoption assistance and allows employees to put up to $5,000 a year in a tax-free account to be used for day care.[15] Other companies with programs to aid would-be adoptive parents are the Microsoft computer company, Wendy's, the fast-food chain, and Ben & Jerry's ice cream.[16] Particularly generous when it comes to giving leave time to new mothers is Home Box Office. HBO develops programming for its own and the Cinemax television movie channels. Company maternity leave generally amounts to two months with pay, and three more, unpaid, months. HBO also offers paternity leave to new fathers.[17]

Flextime and Other Options

Another way businesses have found to help their employees deal with both a job and a family is by being flexible about work schedules and conditions. At some companies, a woman can choose to work three or four days a week instead of five. Some women share a single job with another person—usually also a woman—who also is looking for flexibility. Others work at home part of the time.

Michele Jurkouich, mother of ten-month-old Bryce, is in the latter group. Jurkouich spends three days a week in her office at Merrill Lynch, the financial giant. The other two days, Jurkouich stays home, a pioneer in what has come to be called "telecommuting."

Jurkouich's at-home days aren't just a matter of doing a couple of hours of work in between cleaning house and cuddling Bryce. Her home office is outfitted as professionally as her office at Merrill Lynch. Her telephone number there is the same as at her workplace. Jurkouich, a systems analyst, puts in the same full workday at each location. The only difference is that she avoids a long, tiresome commute two working days each week.

Where did she learn to be so disciplined? At Merrill Lynch. Before Jurkouich adopted her new work schedule, the company put her through four months of applications, interviews, and formal training. The training included two weeks in a telecommuting simulation lab. There, cut off from her fellow workers—as she would be at home—Jurkouich practiced doing her usual work in an unusual setting. Instead of being in her regular windowless cubicle, she was given an office that looked out over several buildings and a patch of woods—just the kind of distracting view she would have at home. Outside her office door in the simulation lab stood a fully stocked refrigerator, as much a temptation to snack breaks there as it would be in her own kitchen. Lab instructors helped Jurkouich develop strategies for heading off, politely but firmly, such potential interruptions as neighbors dropping in to visit or friends calling to chat.

As 1998 began, 500 Merrill Lynch employees, about 1 percent of its workforce, had gone through the lab course and begun their new, flexible working arrangements. The company's work-at-home scheme and its simulation lab are unusual now, but both may become more common as women seek new ways to balance home and career. Other companies exploring flexible scheduling—also known as flextime—are American Express and Fish & Richardson, a New York law firm.[18]

One caveat—warning—about flextime. A woman who takes advantage of it will have to be sure her boss isn't using it as a means of easing her out of a full-time job and into less-well-paid, benefits-poor, part-time work. The same warning applies to other "Mommy Track" work options. Accepting such options as taking months of unpaid leave or being excused from out-of-town travel can derail a woman's career against her wishes.

Another way sympathetic employers can help working women is by loosening certain job rules. Once, for instance, most employers severely restricted workers' use of company telephones for personal calls. Today, many encourage their employees to place calls if they feel the need. Many modern bosses understand that workers are better able to concentrate on the job when they aren't worrying about a sick child or an elderly parent. "There is a general trend toward acknowledging that people need to deal with things in order to be productive," says one Boston consultant. Nor is telephone use limited to workers who have telephones in their offices. Levi Strauss & Company, the clothing manufacturer, found a way to make it easier for factory workers to deal with minor family crises. The company installed more telephones in employee-break rooms.[19]

Employers can also make life less stressful for working women by taking a strong stand against sexual discrimination in the workplace. The majority of U.S. companies have had formal sexual-harassment policies since the late 1980s.[20] For the most part, however, those policies have been geared toward prohibiting lewd comments and unwanted physical contact. They have largely ignored such forms of gender discrimination as the ridiculing of women in general, or the sly sabotaging of their work. Revising policies to focus more on the discrimination aspect of sexual harassment would indicate to workers of both sexes that an employer is serious about achieving workplace equality.

Finally, employers who want to help shatter the glass ceiling can adopt programs aimed at broadening the horizons of present— and future—generations of women. Many businesses sponsor an annual Take-Our-Daughters-to-Work Day as a way to acquaint girls and young women with the variety of jobs that will be open to them as adults. Participants get to see exactly what it is their parents are doing while they are in school or attending after-school programs. At some companies, Take-Our-Daughters-to-Work days have generalized into Take-Our-Children-to-Work events. Either way, the programs encourage young people to start thinking about possible careers while they are still in elementary or middle school.

Another type of program gaining in popularity goes by the name of "mentworking." Mentworking—the word was coined by Beverly Kaye, a career development consultant—is a combination of mentoring and networking. In a mentworking program, older and younger workers are brought together in an informal setting.

The younger workers, who may not be sure exactly what direction they want their careers to take, talk with as many different older workers as possible, learning about various company departments and projects. As friendly relationships develop, younger workers often find themselves with not one but several mentors, each willing to contribute to furthering their careers. Companies with mentworking programs include Hamilton Standard, an aerospace manufacturer in Connecticut, and Trevira, a North Carolina textile company. The city of San Diego has also offered mentworking sessions to some of its employees.[21]

Changing Perspectives

Introducing programs like mentworking, sponsoring Take-Our-Daughters-to-Work days, and instituting broad antidiscrimination policies are some tactics that employers are using to help alter the way women are viewed and treated in the workplace. Other institutions and individuals need to contribute to changing society's perspectives as well. Think, for instance, what the media could do to transform the way women are viewed—and the way they view themselves.

Until now, the media have not always presented the most positive images. According to a study released in 1997, movies, television, and magazines consistently show girls and women as being more concerned about their looks and romances than about their lives as independent human beings. The study was conducted by Dr. Nancy Signorelli of the University of Delaware. She and others examined twenty-three popular TV shows, fifteen movies, three weeks of top-twenty music videos, and four magazines, *YM*, *Sassy*, *Teen*, and *Seventeen*.

The first oddity that the researchers uncovered was that females are underrepresented in the media. Although women make up more than half of the U.S. population, the majority of those depicted in the media are men. On TV 55 percent of characters are male; in the movies that percentage rises to 63 percent. In music videos an astonishing 78 percent of all performers are men.

What were those men doing? On television 41 percent were shown working at a job. Only 28 percent of female TV characters were shown working. In the movies 60 percent of men—and 35 percent of women—were depicted on the job. Of the magazine articles the researchers examined, 35 percent were about dating. Only 12 percent dealt with school or career topics.

"What we are seeing is a constant, cumulative, omnipresent picture," says Lois Salisbury, the president of Children Now, an advocacy group based in Oakland, California. "And it's hard to get away from. A girl could . . . turn off her television, but she's going to get it at the movies. She could decide just to read, but she would have to boycott most popular magazines for girls." She may also have to boycott many of the older books, still in school and public libraries, that present an outdated view of girls and women.

Dr. Jane Brown, a journalism professor at a Southern university, is equally disturbed by the media's habit of showing girls and women as passive, rather than active, and as dependent upon others, rather than as self-confident and self-reliant individuals. "We are where we have always been," she comments. "That is what we were concerned with 20 years ago," Brown adds.[22]

Yet change may be on the way. A new magazine for teenage girls, *Jump*, made its debut in 1997. *Jump* emphasizes athletics. Other newcomers to magazine racks include *Womensport* and *Sports for Women*. Such publications present "a totally fresh look at how women in America view themselves," says Lucy S. Danziger, editor in chief of *Sports for Women*.[23] Nancy Signorelli even found some positives in the way TV and movies depict women. In the television shows she looked at, 34 percent of female characters were shown using their intelligence, and 35 percent were seen as self-reliant. In the movies nearly 70 percent used their intelligence to solve problems.[24] That's a new perspective.

Changing perspectives is also the goal of organizations like the National Science Foundation, the Ford Foundation, and the Carnegie Corporation of New York. These and other groups have joined together to fund Operation SMART. SMART stands for Science, Math and Relevant Technology. Operation SMART is administered by Girls Incorporated, a national network aimed at improving the lives and economic prospects of girls and women.

According to Operation SMART, women will make up 48 percent of the U.S. workforce by 2005. "Unless today's girls acquire the skills they need to survive in the information age," the group's leaders say, "tomorrow's women will remain at the bottom of the wage scale." Determined not to let that happen, Operation SMART invites girls to attend courses and workshops in auto mechanics, geology, veterinary science, and other nontraditional fields. In 1998 the group was serving girls ages six to eighteen in thirty-five states.[25]

WIST—Women Into Science and Technology—is another project whose goal is to interest young women in what will be the high-paid jobs of the twenty-first century. On its Career Activity Day, held at Kean University in Union, New Jersey, WIST invites ninth-grade girls to participate in workshops on statistics, computers, occupational therapy, genetics, oceanography, and other scientific and technical areas.[26]

To be really effective, projects like WIST and Operation SMART will have to gain the full cooperation of school systems, public and private. Traditionally, teachers and administrators have encouraged girls to believe that they can do well only in subjects like reading and English. Boys, the message continues, excel in math and science. The assertion that gender determines academic excellence is as preposterous as the idea that one sex is composed of sugar and spice, the other of snaps and snails. Today, many schools are making conscious efforts to encourage girls to develop their math and science skills.

Changes of perspective are apparent on the university level as well. One comes from the Harvard Business School in Cambridge,

Massachusetts, which is among the nation's most influential in the training of corporate leaders.

At the heart of the school's curriculum are thousands of case studies. Each profiles the career of an actual corporate executive. Students use the case studies to understand how leading executives look at difficult situations, analyze their options, arrive at sound business decisions—and reach the highest levels of success.

Until 1998, virtually all of Harvard's case studies featured a man at the center. When a woman did put in a rare case-study appearance, it was generally as a low-level employee struggling to balance work and family.

Now that has changed. For the first time, the business school is including significant numbers of real-life female executives in its case-study files. From now on, Harvard business students will be seeing women as creative individuals building successful careers. They will be seeing women, not as secretaries, assistants, and middle managers but as living models of the powerful corporate executives in whose footsteps they hope one day to follow. Harvard Business School students—one-third of whom are women—will be learning what it takes to break through the glass ceiling.[27]

Then they'll be ready to go out into the world and break through it themselves.

8

READY . . .
GET SET . . .

How does a person prepare to break through the glass ceiling? The first answer— "go out and play"—may come as a surprise. Playing sports is fun. It is, as it turns out, also one of the best things anyone can do to prepare for success.

Benita Fitzgerald Mosley was "kind of tall and lanky" as a seventh grader. Her self-esteem was low. "We weren't the nerds," she says now of herself and her friends. "But we weren't the popular cheerleader-type either. . . . We were trying to find our place."

Benita found her place on the junior-high track team in Dale City, Virginia. In her eighth-grade year, she was a district champion. She graduated from high school with a full four-year scholarship to the University of Tennessee. In 1984 Benita won an Olympic gold medal in the 100-meter hurdles for women. Today, she is president of the Women's Sports Foundation (W.S.F.) and director of the U.S. Olympic Training Center in Chula Vista, California.

"You gain a base of strength [from playing sports] that you carry with you the rest of your life," Mosley says. Studies confirm her view. A survey conducted by the Women's Sports Foundation showed female athletes scoring higher on standardized tests than female nonathletes. Another W.S.F. survey indicates that female athletes are more likely than nonathletes to graduate from high school. A third study, this one by the National Collegiate Athletic Association, revealed a similar phenomenon at the college level. Among U.S. black women college students overall, the graduation rate is 41 percent. Among black women college athletes, the rate rises to 58 percent.

Mosley can relate to the findings of these studies. She is black. She also holds a degree from the University of Tennessee. And she attributes much of her success to the athletic training she started in seventh grade. That training gave her the discipline and self-esteem she has been building on ever since.

Others agree that participating in sports may constitute the best possible foundation for future achievement, especially for girls. "The physical strength, competence and sense of mastery in sports help girls," says one woman. It gives them the feeling of self-assurance that comes more automatically to boys. It enables girls to get off on a more equal footing in life.[1]

What else can girls—and boys—do to lay the groundwork for future achievement? Some suggestions:

• Stay in school. The more education you have, the more jobs— and the more good jobs—will be open to you. Studies uniformly show that on average, high-school graduates earn more than nongraduates. College graduates earn more than those who left school after grade twelve. Those who hold advanced degrees earn still more.

• Get as much mathematical, scientific, and technological training as possible. The Operation SMART people are right. Many of the highest-paying jobs of the twenty-first century will be in scientific and technical fields. Betty Vetter's research for the National Science Foundation showed that women who have studied college-level math come closest to equaling men's salaries. Vetter calls this tidbit of information a "well-kept secret."[2] Benita Fitzgerald Mosley's college degree, incidentally, is in industrial engineering.

- Learn what's out there. Take advantage of workshops and courses offered by groups like Operation SMART and Women Into Science and Technology. (Search the Internet for information about upcoming events in your area.) Visit a real-life workplace on a Take-Our-Daughters (or Children)-to-Work Day. If your parents' employers don't sponsor such a program, find a working friend or relative whose employer does. Ask if you can participate.

- Check out organizations like the Scouts, 4H, and Boys' and Girls' Clubs. Many have developed mentoring programs that give young people a chance to interact with working professionals on a one-to-one basis. Ask your school guidance director about Career Fairs or similar events.

- Volunteer—and learn marketable skills. Show up at a Red Cross or Salvation Army shelter after a natural disaster like a hurricane or a flood. You may be asked to cook or serve meals, set up cots for sleeping, organize games for children, or lead a sing-along. It's all good experience. You may even pick up some pointers on administrative work. Sign up with Habitat for Humanity, whose volunteers build homes for families who could not otherwise afford them. Carpentry skills are always valuable.

- Consult your interests. Love to read? You may want to think about becoming a librarian or working in a bookstore. Like the outdoors? Maybe you'll want to join the Forest Service. Yearn to travel? You could become an airline pilot or flight attendant. You could be a tour guide or open a travel agency. You could write for a travel magazine or edit travel books.

- Be creative. You may dream of a career in health care. Becoming a nurse may sound easier than aiming for an M.D. degree. But are those the only options? What about training as an occupational therapist, or in sports medicine? What about massage or osteopathy? If you like clothes and makeup, you could get a job in a boutique or behind the cosmetic counter in a department store. Or you could sign up at an art school and try for a career in fashion design.

- Be flexible. Even though you personally don't know anyone who teaches college, it doesn't mean you can't become a professor. Never seen a female firefighter? It doesn't matter. They're out there, and you can be among them.

- Do some research. What are the most promising jobs? Magazines aimed at an audience of working women publish yearly ten-best lists. According to *Working Mother*, the 1998 leaders included occupational therapist, registered nurse, physician's assistant, social worker, computer network architect or systems analyst, teacher, employee trainer, financial planner, and public-relations specialist.[3] What's on this year's list?

How does a person break through the glass ceiling? Think about Brenda Berkman, who took the New York City Fire Department to court to win her job. Or about Sheila Connors, doorwoman, who forced the news media to pay attention to her story. Remember the women who resisted Home Depot's unfair hiring and promotion policies. Picture police rookie Jane Perlov crashing through that drug-den door.

Ready . . . Get Set . . . Go!

SOURCE NOTES

Chapter 1

1. Grondin, Joyce, "Nash Teacher 'Got the Best Job There Ever Was,'" *Capital Weekly* (Augusta, ME), August 28, 1997, p. 1.

2. Russell, Jan Jarboe, "Affairs of State," *Working Woman*, November/December 1996, p. 29.

3. *The World Almanac:1998*, K-III Reference Corporation, Mahwah, NJ.

4. Aburdene, Patricia and John Naisbitt, *Megatrends for Women: From Liberation to Leadership*, Fawcett Columbine, New York, 1992, p. 343.

5. Morrison, Ann M., Randall P. White, and Ellen Van Velsor, *Breaking the Glass Ceiling: Can Women Reach the Top of America's Largest Corporations?* Addison-Wesley Publishing Company, Inc., Reading, MA, 1987, p. 6.

6. Dobrzynski, Judith H., "Linda Wachner: The First Woman to Buy and Head a Fortune 1000 Company," *Working Woman*, November/December 1996, p. 108.

7. Chaikin, Andrew, "Sally Ride: The First American Woman in Space," *Working Woman*, November/December 1996, p. 42.

8. Broad, William J., "A Tiny Rover, Built on the Cheap, Is Ready to Explore Distant Mars," *The New York Times*, July 5, 1997, p. 7.

9. Chaikin, Andrew, p. 42.

10. Morrison, Ann M., p. 13.

11. Lewin, Tamar, "Women Losing Ground to Men In Widening Income Difference," *The New York Times*, September 15, 1997, A1.

12. "Forget All That Bad Publicity: A Woman's Place Is in the Air Force," *The New York Times*, September 10, 1997, B6.

13. Pollitt, Katha, "Go Figure," *The Nation*, April 14, 1997, p. 9.

14. Vetter, Betty M., *What Is Holding Up the Glass Ceiling? Barriers to Women in the Science and Engineering Workforce*, adapted by the author from an article to be published by the National Science Foundation, Fall, 1992, issue of MOSAIC, 3.

15. "Hurtful Hints," *The New York Times Magazine*, June 1, 1997.

Chapter 2

1. Leviticus 27: 1-7.

2. Anderson, Bonnie S., and Judith P. Zinsser, *A History of Their Own: Women in Europe from Prehistory to the Present*, Harper & Row, Publishers, New York, 1988, Vol. I, p. 41.

3. Ibid., p. 27.

4. Ehrenberg, Margaret, *Women in Prehistory*, University of Oklahoma Press, Norman, OK, 1989, p. 12.

5. Ibid., pp. 52-53.

6. Ibid., p. 19.

7. Ibid., p. 42.

8. Ibid., p. 14.

9. Ibid., pp. 105-106.

10. Anderson, Bonnie S., and Judith P. Zinsser, *A History of Their Own: Women in Europe from Prehistory to the Present*, Harper & Row, Publishers, New York, 1988, Vol. II, p. xii.

11. Anderson, Bonnie S., Vol. I, p. 277.

12. Ibid., p. 495.

13. Ibid., p. 277.

14. Ibid., p. 322.

15. Ehrenberg, Margaret, p. 167.

16. Anderson, Bonnie S., Vol. I, pp. 151-156.

17. Ibid., p. 362.
18. Ibid., p. 361.
19. Ibid., pp. 371-372.
20. Ibid., pp. 289-290.
21. Anderson, Bonnie S., Vol. II, pp. 341, 161.
22. Johnson, Anne E., "Before the Renaissance, A Renaissance Woman," *The New York Times*, September 28, 1997, Section 2, p. 27.
23. Anderson, Bonnie S., Vol. I, p. 360.
24. Ibid., pp.131-132.
25. Ibid., p. 324.
26. Anderson, Bonnie S., Vol. II, p. xviii.
27. Ibid., p. 116.
28. Ibid., p. 149.
29. Ibid., p. xviii.
30. Ibid., p. 141.
31. Ibid., pp. 253-254.
32. Ibid., pp. 249-250.

Chapter 3

1. Berkin, Carol, *First Generations: Women in Colonial America*, Hill and Wang, New York, 1996, pp. 79-81.
2. Ibid., p. 87.
3. Ibid., p. 58.
4. Ibid., pp. 61-62.
5. Ehrenberg, Margaret, *Women in Prehistory*, University of Oklahoma Press, Norman, OK, 1989, p. 98.
6. Berkin, Carol, p. 63.
7. Ehrenberg, Margaret, p. 64.
8. Schlesinger, Arthur M., Jr., General Editor, *The Almanac of American History*, The Putnam Publishing Group, New York, 1983, p. 79.
9. Berkin, Carol, pp. 111, 120-121.
10. Schlesinger, Arthur M., Jr., p. 276.
11. Ibid., p. 255.

12. Ibid., p 210.

13. Ibid., p. 316.

14. Ibid., p. 369.

15. Ibid., p. 419.

16. Garraty, John A., Ed., *The Young Reader's Companion to American History*, Houghton Mifflin Company, Boston, 1994, p. 307.

17. Schlesinger, Arthur M., Jr., p. 432.

18. Anderson, Bonnie S., and Judith P. Zinsser, *A History of Their Own: Women in Europe from Prehistory to the Present*, Harper & Row, Publishers, New York, 1988, Vol. II, p. 200.

19. Ibid., p. 201.

20. Ibid., p. 261.

21. Ibid., pp. 146-147.

22. Ibid., pp. 201-202.

23. Ibid., p. 207.

24. Schlesinger, Arthur M., Jr., pp. 488-489.

25. Aburdene, Patricia, and John Naisbitt, *Megatrends for Women: From Liberation to Leadership*, Fawcett Columbine, New York, 1992, p. 30.

26. Schlesinger, Arthur M., Jr., p. 495.

27. Marcano, Tony, "Famed Riveter in War Effort, Rose Monroe, Dies at 77," *The New York Times*, June 2, 1997, B13.

28. Schlesinger, Arthur M., Jr., p. 590.

Chapter 4

1. Schlesinger, Arthur M., Jr., General Editor, *The Almanac of American History*, The Putnam Publishing Group, New York, 1983, p. 511.

2. Garraty, John A., Ed., *The Young Reader's Companion to American History*, Houghton Mifflin Company, Boston, 1994, p. 349.

3. Schlesinger, Arthur M., Jr., p. 511.

4. Garraty, John A., p. 332.

5. Friedan, Betty, *The Feminine Mystique*, Bantam Doubleday Dell Publishing Group, New York, 1983, pp. 15-16.

6. Ibid., p. 16.

7. Ibid., p. ix.

8. Toobin, Jeffrey, "The Trouble With Sex," *The New Yorker*, February 9, 1998, p. 48.

9. Friedan, Betty, p. 383.

10. Ibid., p. 387.

11. Ibid., p. 387.

12. Garraty, John A., p. 310.

13. Ibid., p. 310.

14. Friedan, Betty, p. 391.

15. Schlesinger, Arthur M., Jr., p. 609.

16. Aburdene, Patricia, and John Naisbitt, *Megatrends for Women: From Liberation to Leadership*, Fawcett Columbine, New York, 1992, p. 242.

17. Garraty, John A., p. 239.

18. *Working Woman*, November/December, 1996.

19. "Former Head of Boston's Airport Is to Be Named Aviation Chief," *The New York Times*, April 30, 1997, A19.

20. *Working Woman.*

21. Aburdene, Patricia, p. 28.

22. *Working Woman.*

23. Aburdene, Patricia, p. 49.

24. Wise, Mike, "Female Refs Say They Owe Their Jobs to Their Ability," *The New York Times*, October 30, 1997, C1.

Chapter 5

1. Cohen, Richard, "Glass Ceiling Dept.," *The New Yorker*, September 29, 1997, p. 33.

2. Barron, James, "Opening Door, Plaza Hotel Makes Woman a Doorman," *The New York Times*, December 6, 1997, B3.

3. Hirschfeld, Neal, "In the Line of Fire," *Good Housekeeping*, November, 1997, p. 27.

4. Ojito, Mirta, "New Post Is Another First For a Female Police Officer," *The New York Times*, December 7, 1997, p. 44.

5. Davidson, Marilyn J., and Cary L. Cooper, *Shattering the Glass Ceiling—The Woman Manager*, Paul Chapman Publishing Ltd., London, 1992, p. 83.

6. Goodnough, Abby, "For Women, a Thin Blue Line," *The New York Times*, August 7, 1997, B1.

7. Vetter, Betty M., *What Is Holding Up the Glass Ceiling? Barriers to Women in the Science and Engineering Workforce*, adapted by the author from an article to be published by the National Science Foundation, Fall, 1992, issue of MOSAIC, pp. 1, 9.

8. Ibid., p. 11.

9. Ibid., p. 9.

10. Davidson, Marilyn J., p. 3.

11. *The World Almanac:1998*, K-III Reference Corporation, Mahwah, NJ, p. 144.

12. Davidson, Marilyn J., p. 7.

13. Stout, Hilary, "This Investment Fund Pries Loose Some Cash For Female-Run Firms," *The Wall Street Journal*, November 28, 1997, B4.

14. Goodstein, Laurie, "Unusual, But Not Unorthodox," *The New York Times*, February 6, 1998, B1.

15. Aburdene, Patricia, and John Naisbitt, *Megatrends for Women: From Liberation to Leadership*, Fawcett Columbine, New York, 1992, p. 135.

16. Wayne, Leslie, and Kenneth N. Gilpin, "Avon Calls on a Man to Lead It," *The New York Times*, December 12, 1997, D1.

17. Ibid.

18. Vetter, Betty M., p. 10.

19. Ibid., pp. 14-16.

20. *The World Almanac:1998*, K-III Reference Corporation, Mahwah, NJ, p. 144.

21. Lewin, Tamar, "Equal Pay for Equal Work Is No. 1 Goal of Women," *The New York Times*, September 5, 1997, A20.

22. Pollitt, Katha, "Go Figure," *The Nation*, April 14, 1997, p. 9.

23. Lewin, Tamar, "Women Losing Ground to Men In Widen-

ing Income Difference," *The New York Times*, September 15, 1997, A1.

24. Morrison, Ann M., Randall P. White, and Ellen Van Velsor, *Breaking the Glass Ceiling: Can Women Reach the Top of America's Largest Corporations?*, Addison-Wesley Publishing Company, Inc., Reading, MA, 1987, p. 64.

25. Vetter, Betty M., p. 8.

26. Lewin, Tamar, "Equal Pay for Equal Work Is No. 1 Goal of Women."

27. Meredith, Robyn, "Strip Clubs Under Siege as Salesman's Haven," *The New York Times*, September 20, 1997, D1.

28. Morrison, p. 64.

29. Truell, Peter, "Another Year, Another Bundle," *The New York Times*, December 5, 1997, D1.

30. Waldman, Amy, "Labor's New Face," *The Nation*, September 22, 1977, p. 11.

Chapter 6

1. Deogun, Nikhil, "Top PepsiCo Executive Picks Family Over Job," *The Wall Street Journal*, September 24, 1997.

2. "Family Values Win," *The New York Times*, September 28, 1997, Sec. 3, p. 2.

3. Goldberg, Carey, "A Murder Trial About More Than a Nanny," *The New York Times*, October 24, 1997, A18.

4. Pollitt, Katha, "Killer Moms, Working Nannies," *The Nation*, November 24, 1997, p. 9.

5. Holcomb, Betty, "What's Best for Babies?," *Good Housekeeping*, June 1998, p. 179.

6. *The World Almanac:1998*, K-III Reference Corporation, Mahwah, NJ, p. 376.

7. Rimer, Sara, "Children of Working Poor Are Day Care's Forgotten," *The New York Times*, November 25, 1997, A1.

8. Drape, Joe, "Baby on Board," *The New York Times*, August 3, 1997, Sec. 8, p. 1.

9. Rimer, Sara.

10. Jordano, Rosemary and Marie Oates, "Putting the Children First," *The New York Times*, November 9, 1997, Sec. 3, p. 19.

11. Rimer, Sara.

12. Jordano, Rosemary.

13. Rimer, Sara.

14. Dobrzynski, Judith H., "Judge Splits on Issues and Money in G.E. Executive's Divorce Case," *The New York Times*, December 4, 1997, D1.

15. Davidson, Marilyn J., and Cary L. Cooper, *Shattering the Glass Ceiling—The Woman Manager*, Paul Chapman Publishing Ltd., London, 1992, p. 10.

16. Barron, James, "Former New Yorker Executive Sues Magazine," *The New York Times*, October 23, 1997, B12.

17. Lublin, Joann, "How One Woman Manages In World of Male Directors," *The Wall Street Journal*, November 28, 1997, B1.

18. Ojito, Mirta, "New Post Is Another First For a Female Police Officer," *The New York Times*, December 7, 1997, p. 44.

19. Weiss, Ann E., *Money Games: The Business of Sports*, Houghton Mifflin Company, Boston, 1993.

20. Aburdene, Patricia, and John Naisbitt, *Megatrends for Women: From Liberation to Leadership*, Fawcett Columbine, New York, 1992, pp. 40-45.

21. Vetter, Betty M., *What Is Holding Up the Glass Ceiling? Barriers to Women in the Science and Engineering Workforce*, adapted by the author from an article to be published by the National Science Foundation, Fall, 1992, issue of MOSAIC, p. 12.

22. Morrison, Ann M., Randall P. White, and Ellen Van Velsor, *Breaking the Glass Ceiling: Can Women Reach the Top of America's Largest Corporations?*, Addison-Wesley Publishing Company, Inc., Reading, MA, 1987, pp. 48-52.

23. Davidson, Marilyn J., p. 46.

24. Dreifus, Claudia, "Love Soft as an Easy Chair (Cue the Violins)," *The New York Times*, November 11, 1997, E1.

25. Chaikin, Andrew, "Sally Ride: The First American Woman in Space," *Working Woman*, November/December 1996, p. 42.

26. Morrison, Ann M., p. 100.

27. Ibid., pp. 15-17.

28. Davidson, Marilyn J., p. 86.

29. Shellenbarger, Sue, "Woman's Resignation From Top Pepsi Post Rekindles Debates," *The Wall Street Journal*, October 8, 1997, B1.

30. Davidson, Marilyn J., p. 88.

31. Hirschfeld, Neal, "In the Line of Fire," *Good Housekeeping*, November, 1997, p. 27.

32. Waldman, Amy, "Labor's New Face," *The Nation*, September 22, 1997, p. 11.

33. Anderson, Bonnie S., and Judith P. Zinsser, *A History of Their Own: Women in Europe from Prehistory to the Present*, Harper & Row, Publishers, New York, 1988, Vol. II, p. 259.

34. Aburdene, Patricia, p. 130.

35. Morrison, Ann M., p. 82.

36. Aburdene, Patricia, p. 95.

37. Vetter, Betty M., p. 13.

38. Shenon, Philip, "Army's Leadership Blamed in Report On Sexual Abuses," *The New York Times*, September 12, 1997, A1

39. Toobin, Jeffrey, "The Trouble With Sex," *The New Yorker*, February 9, 1998, p. 48.

40. Gilpin, Kenneth N., "Firm to Pay $10 Million in Settlement Of Sex Case," *The New York Times*, February 6, 1998, A16.

41. "Pilot's Award Reduced In Harassment Case," *The New York Times*, February 2, 1998, B6.

42. Toobin, Jeffrey.

Chapter 7

1. Gilpin, Kenneth N., "Firm to Pay $10 Million in Settlement Of Sex Case," *The New York Times*, February 6, 1998, A16.

2. Myerson, Allen R., "Home Depot Pays $87.5 Million For

Not Promoting More Women," *The New York Times*, September 20, 1997, A7.

3. Garraty, John A., Ed., *The Young Reader's Companion to American History*, Houghton Mifflin Company, Boston, 1994, p. 15.

4. Rosen, Jeffrey, "Damage Control," *The New Yorker*, February 23–March 2, 1998, p. 58.

5. Golden, Tim, "California's Ban on Preferences Goes into Effect," *The New York Times*, August 29, 1997, A1.

6. "Affirmative Actions," *The Nation*, November 24, 1997, p. 4.

7. Verhovek, Sam Howe, "In Poll, Americans Reject Means But Not Ends of Racial Diversity," *The New York Times*, December 14, 1997, p. 1.

8. Chambers, Marcia, "For Women, 25 Years of Title IX Has Not Leveled the Playing Field," *The New York Times*, June 16, 1997, A1.

9. "Gender Equity in College Sports," *The New York Times*, April 30, 1997, A20.

10. Mitchell, Elizabeth, "Family Leave Act Pays Off," *Capital Weekly* (Augusta, ME), November 13, 1997, A9.

11. Seelye, Katharine Q., "Clinton Proposes $21 Billion Over 5 Years for Child Care," *The New York Times*, January 8, 1998, A1.

12. Myers, Steven Lee, "Panel's Advice on Troops Is Attacked," *The New York Times*, December 17, 1997, A26.

13. Wayne, Leslie, and Kenneth N. Gilpin, "Avon Calls On a Man to Lead It," *The New York Times*, December 12, 1997, D1.

14. Greenhouse, Steven, "Nike Supports Women in Its Ads But Not Its Factories, Groups Say," *The New York Times*, October 26, 1997, p. 30.

15. Internet site: women.com

16. Kelley, Tina, "In Adoption, New Help From Employers," *The New York Times*, November 16, 1997, Section 3, p. 11.

17. women.com

18. Johnson, Kirk, "Limits on the Work-at-Home Life," *The New York Times*, December 17, 1997, B1.

19. Bray, John, "The Office Phone Vs. the Tug of Home," *The New York Times*, December 21, 1997, Section 3, p. 9.

20. Davidson, Marilyn J., and Cary L. Cooper, *Shattering the Glass Ceiling—The Woman Manager*, Paul Chapman Publishing Ltd., London, 1992, p. 112.

21. Lawlor, Julia, "Mentoring Meets Networking In Formal Programs," *The New York Times*, November 30, 1997, Section 3, p. 8.

22. Smith, Dinitia, "Media More Likely to Show Women Talking About Romance Than at a Job, Study Says," *The New York Times*, May 1, 1997, B15.

23. Pogrebin, Robin, "Adding Sweat and Muscle to a Familiar Formula," *The New York Times*, September 21, 1997, Section 3, p. 1.

24. Smith, Dinitia.

25. Internet site: http://www.girlsinc.org or http://www.girlsinc.org/programs/smart.htm/

26. Internet site: wistproj@turbo.kean.edu

27. Hays, Constance L., "Focus for M.B.A.'s Turns to Women," *The New York Times*, November 14, 1997, A14.

Chapter 8

1. Kiernan, Denise, "Word May Be Out, But Schoolgirls Need to Get Message," *The New York Times*, June 22, 1997, Section 8, p. 8.

2. Vetter, Betty M., *What Is Holding Up the Glass Ceiling? Barriers to Women in the Science and Engineering Workforce*, adapted by the author from an article to be published by the National Science Foundation, Fall, 1992, issue of MOSAIC, p. 3.

3. Cheney, Karen, "10 Hottest Careers for Working Moms," *Working Mother*, April, 1998, p. 24.

FOR FURTHER READING

Bland, Celia. *The Mechanical Age: The Industrial Revolution in England*. New York: Facts on File, 1995.

Blau, Justine. *Betty Friedan: Feminist*. Broomall, PA: Chelsea House, 1990.

Bolden, Tonya. *And Not Afraid to Dare: The Stories of Ten African-American Women*. New York: Scholastic, 1998.

Brown, Gene. *The Struggle to Grow: Expansionism and Industrialization (1880-1913)*. Brookfield, CT: Twenty-First Century Books, 1993.

Colman, Penny. *Rosie the Riveter: Women Working on the Home Front in World War II*. New York: Crown, 1995.

Garza, Hedda. *Barred from the Bar: A History of Women in the Legal Profession*. Danbury, CT: Franklin Watts, 1996.

Greenberg, Keith Elliot. *Stunt Woman: Daredevil Specialist*. Woodbridge, CT: Blackbirch Press, 1996.

Harvey, Miles. *Women's Voting Rights*. Danbury, CT: Children's Press, 1996.

Lindop, Laurie. *Dynamic Modern Women* series: *Athletes, Champions of Equality, Political Leaders, Scientists and Doctors*. Brookfield, CT: Twenty-First Century Books, 1996-1997.

Nicholson, Lois P. *Oprah Winfrey*. Broomall, PA: Chelsea House, 1997.

Shell, Barry. *Great Canadian Scientists*. Custer, WA: Orca Book Publishers, 1998.

Stille, Darlene R. *Extraordinary Women Scientists*. Danbury, CT: Children's Press, 1995.

Wooten, Sara McIntosh. *Martha Stewart: America's Lifestyle Expert*. Woodbridge, CT: Blackbirch Press, 1998.

Zeinert, Karen. *Those Incredible Women of World War II*. Brookfield, CT: The Millbrook Press, 1994.

INDEX

125